AssociationHelpNow™
Condo/HOA Primer

Raymond Dickey

Brainerd Communications, Inc. • Atlantic City, New Jersey

Copyright ©2014 by Brainerd Communications, Inc.
All rights reserved. No part of this book may be reproduced in any form, electronic or mechanical, without written permission from the publisher.

Michigan AssociationHelpNow™ Condo/HOA Primer
ISBN 978-0-9860904-0-0

Cover photos ©iStockphoto.com

Published by Brainerd Communications, Inc., 1 Convention Blvd., Suite 2, #285, Atlantic City, NJ 08401. Printed in the USA.

Readers are responsible for any actions taken in relation to the content of this book. Brainerd Communications, Inc. recommends that readers take additional steps to educate themselves outside of this publication, before using the information contained within, as well as consulting with their own professionals to decide any course of action for themselves, their companies or associations.

Contents

Forward 4

1. Covenants, Conditions & Restrictions (CC&Rs) 7
2. Collection of Delinquent Dues 25
3. The Association's Records 39
4. Association Board Member Elections 43
5. The Fair Housing Act & Civil Rights 49
6. Transitions 57
7. Construction Defects 59
8. Reserve Studies 63
9. Association Loans 75
10. Association Insurance — Ensuring You're Protected 81
11. Association Accounting & Budgets 97
12. Financial Management, Nuts & Bolts on Budgeting and Financial Warning Signs 107
13. Calculating Association Assessments 113
14. Association Board Meetings 119
15. Working With and Motivating Volunteers on the Board and Committees 123
16. Disaster Preparation 131
17. After the Disaster — Restoration of the Association ... 139
18. The Association's Roofs 147

Glossary 153

Source Bios 157

Forward

By Michele Newman,
Publishing Coordinator, Brainerd Communications, Inc.

Nearly two decades of publishing in the community association industry provided the catalyst to create this book. Raymond Dickey's company, Brainerd Communications, Inc. has published many different types of industry periodicals, however, even though considered a niche publishing market, community associations represent more than merely a small segment of the country's population. "The community association industry affects the lives of so many people, and the number of individuals residing in HOAs and condominium associations is growing every year," said Dickey.

Over three years ago, Brainerd Communications, Inc. launched its AssociationHelpNow™ website and publications. Since then, Dickey was amazed by the flood of questions, letters and requests by association board members for these publications. Although there are many resources and organizations serving the community association industry, those affected by association operations are eager to learn as much as they can about issues affecting their homes, real estate investments and neighborhoods. As independent resources, these media venues provide readers with valuable information they can use, as they consult with their professionals on the many topics that have arisen in the condo and HOA arena.

This book is not a replacement for professional counsel or advice, however those interviewed in the making of this book introduce a variety of information so board members and homeowners don't need to go into situations cold, but with a basis of knowledge to make informed decisions, along with their professional advisors. "This book shares the insights of industry leaders in the readers' geographic area, so those who read this book learn a common background of information. This book is also a wake-up call to those living in HOAs and condominium associations, that they should stay up-to-date on what's going on in their communities and legislatively as it affects the places where they live," said Dickey. "In addition to this book and other publications, there are many industry associations and private groups that offer ongoing education and information on these topics as well. Residents and investors don't need to feel they are out there alone," he said.

As this book offers a primer for the main topics affecting associations, readers should stay informed by visiting our website, www.AssociationHelpNow.com, and continuing to read everything out there, as this industry has an ever-changing landscape. "As a greater number of people are living in common interest communities, of course the laws affecting them are constantly changing," said Dickey. He emphasized that all people living in these communities, even if they don't become actively involved, should at least know what's going on with their board and the industry at large. "This is the best way to foster harmony in these neighborhoods, as people should be aware they have a 'common interest' in their associations," he said.

1

Covenants, Conditions and Restrictions (CC&Rs)

How are the elements of a community defined? What establishes the components of the common areas versus homeowner-owned areas? Where is it written that certain elements are the responsibility of the homeowner and others the responsibility of the association? These issues and others are established in what's called an association's Covenants, Conditions and Restrictions (CC&Rs). Attorney Mark Makower, of Makower Abbate PLLC in Farmington Hills, Michigan spoke with us at length and explained the nuances of CC&Rs as well as many other important common interest community topics. One important note — in Michigan, as well as some other states, statutes are different for condominiums versus homeowner associations (HOAs). That is something to keep in mind for nearly all aspects of association governance and living.

Makower explained that CC&Rs typically refer to an eponymous document called the declaration of covenants, conditions and restrictions, which is recorded against property in a subdivision. It's a title that is in general use for a document that contains restrictive covenants — or use restrictions. Sometimes, in jurisdictions other than Michigan, this title is also given to a document of restrictive covenants in a condominium. However, in Michigan, the document that serves this purpose in a condominium is called the Master Deed.

CC&Rs are traditionally recorded as land becomes subject to them through filing with the county register of deeds office.

Now, CC&Rs should not be confused with the rules and regulations of an association. Rules and regulations are something different entirely. Most distinctively, boards can generally change rules and regulations without holding a vote of the association's members — the CC&Rs cannot be changed in this manner. Rules and regulations deal more with the more hum-drum details of daily life, such as when the trash is allowed at the curb and what items are restricted from being placed on balconies. However the rules and regulations work in conjunction with the CC&Rs. How so? First, Makower noted a distinction between how these work in condominiums versus HOAs. He explained that rules and regulations are statutorily recognized in condominiums in the State of Michigan. They are not statutorily recognized in HOAs that utilize a declaration of CC&Rs. So whether or not a board has rule power at all is going to depend on whether there is a grant of power to pass rules in the declaration itself. At that point the declaration is going to govern the breadth of that rule making power and the depth of rules and regulations that can actually be issued.

In condominiums, where it is provided by statute — that is, state law — the rules and regulations have been determined by various court cases in Michigan to apply to what are referred to as *de minimis* aspects of daily life, and to clarify grants of discretion given to the governing body. "If you have a restriction, for instance, that says you shall not do 'this' unless you get the approval of the board of directors or the approval of the architectural control committee, the rules and regulations can establish under what circumstances you can do 'this.' And under what circumstances the association or committee will approve whatever 'this' is. That is a clarification of a grant of discretion," Makower said.

The *de minimus* aspect of the daily life component of rules and regulations is very similar to the clarification of a grant of discretion. "For instance, no unsightly condition shall be maintained anywhere in the condominium project or within the subdivisions or within the common area," said Makower. The rules and regulations can actually specify what is determined to be an unsightly condition. It can deal with regulating when residents can place their garbage out for pick-up and when the containers need to be brought back.

These types of details that clarify substantive restrictions are what rules and regulations are for. Rules and regulations cannot establish substantive restrictions. Since they are not recorded or voted upon, you can't use rules and regulations to fill gaps or needs where you don't have a grant of discretion already relating to the context in question. "A classic example of that would be if you have no restriction whatsoever on the keeping of pets in your complex. The rules and regulations cannot say, 'We are not going to allow pets,'" Makower said. Something like that requires an amendment of the declaration or the condominium bylaws to establish the substantive restriction. "There are limits to what you can and cannot do. The reason why rules are limited in that way is that they are changeable by the board of directors. They do not generally require a vote of the co-owners and a subsequent board that comes into office can change a previous policy or the rules and regulations at will. Therefore, there is a certain fluidity to rules and regulations that doesn't exist in the governing documents themselves that have the substantive restrictions which require, almost in all cases, some type of super majority vote by the people subject to them to change them," Makower said.

Which governing document carries the most weight in an association? If you're looking for how an association operates, articles of incorporation are number one. Bylaws are number two.

If you're talking about restrictions on use of property, you're going to be talking about the declaration of restrictions in a subdivision or HOA sense and talking about the master deed and condominium bylaws in a condominium sense. "Often times people think the master deed, bylaws and condominium subdivision plan are all different things, and to some extent they are. But they're all exhibits of the master deed in the State of Michigan," Makower said.

When referring to the master deed, you're referring to three separate parts of the master deed in conjunction with one another:
-the Master Deed itself
-the condominium bylaws
-the condominium subdivision plan

Makower explained that they're all the same document. When you talk about which one carries more weight, they are all equal.

How detailed do the CC&Rs need to be in the governing documents? According to Makower, older CC&Rs mainly concerned themselves with a list of building restrictions. More modern declarations deal with several different items. In addition to the architectural restrictions, there are easements noted and granted. In cases where you have shared recreational facilities, the CC&Rs specify the usage of those facilities.

"Obviously you're going to have provisions saying there shall be an administering entity and giving it certain powers and referring to its by-laws for its operational guidelines," said Makower. If an association is funded through assessments or dues, there need to be detailed provisions setting up a covenant providing for those assessments and their enforcement. "Many people think that can be covered in the bylaws of an HOA, and that's incorrect. They cannot be covered in the bylaws of an HOA. It needs to be covered in the substantive recorded restrictions. Otherwise you don't have the types of rights you need to enforce those assessment obligations against the owners of the property," Makower said. The existence of a statutory framework for assessments in condominium projects, on the other hand, makes them entirely different and allows such matters to be covered in the master deed and condominium bylaws.

It must also be specified how the association may change those restrictions from time to time. Those are the components of a good set of CC&Rs. Of course, the needs are dependent on what the association is going to take care of. "If it's simply a roadway, you're going to have a lot less. If it's recreational facilities, parks and docks, you're going to have a lot more. It's all community driven," Makower said.

Vague Language in Governing Documents

One potential problem with governing documents is the use of vague language. On this topic, Makower explained that the biggest issue with vague language is that it's subject to a number of interpretations. Anytime you're talking about a number of different interpretations, you're eventually looking at a judge determining which interpretation is accurate.

"The folks in the black robes use what are called Maxims of Legislative Construction or Contractual Construction in order to determine 'the intent of the drafter of the document,'" Makower said. There are a lot of different considerations that go into trying to determine what a vague provision means. "You have to look throughout the entire document and all related documents to try to ascertain what the person drafting this probably meant given the entire restrictive scheme in which this document operates," he said.

There are many judicial rules and maxims by which these interpretations are made. One example, he explained, is that you don't construe any provision as a nullity. "Everything is assumed to have some type of meaning, so you have to try to fit it into the regulatory scheme so it makes some type of sense. It's a very difficult process — it's a costly process because it must be done in court," he said.

There are situations where vague language cannot be construed. "No matter how you look, there are too many contradictions and no way to harmonize that language with anything that makes sense," he explained. "From a practical standpoint it is much easier to take your vague language and amend it." Makower stressed that doing that is less costly, and it also ensures that the document reflects the needs of the community at that given time.

Challenging the Governing Documents

If boards follow their rules and documents, does the potential exist for them to be challenged successfully?

"Yes, at least here in Michigan, all recorded regulations are subject to what is called the rule of reason," he said. In other words, just because something is in the rules and regulations, it does not mean it's necessarily enforceable. There must be some useful purpose being served by a particular regulation. It should be as unobtrusive as possible to achieve the means of the regulation. And it must not violate any other law or regulation by which the community that it is imposed upon is governed.

As an example: "A restriction, which you'll find very often in quite a few older documents pertains to approval of satellite dishes of all kinds within condominium associations or homeowners associations. If you apply that restriction because it's there, yes, it can be very successfully challenged because you have an overriding governmental policy established by the FCC Rules and Orders saying you can't restrict certain dishes no matter what type of organization you are, including municipalities," Makower said.

Even though such a rule may be written, it would be unenforceable. The definition of a single-family is another such rule. "They may seem to be reasonable on their face. The board will try to enforce them and find itself staring a civil rights complaint right in the face because it violates the Fair Housing Act," he said.

Many scenarios come up where a rule is written, but it is not enforceable. Usually the reason is due to a governmental preemption or discriminatory results achieved through the provision. "Those are two of the largest groups of things that render something unreasonable," he said.

Alternatively, a provision can be unenforceable simply in the way it has been drafted. "If it's against public policy, it can be struck down for that reason," he said. An example of this could be someone wanting to reduce their carbon footprint by being allowed to use a clothesline in an HOA where clotheslines are prohibited in the rules.

"If you go to some of the states that are a little more proactive on these types of things, you probably will find judges that will declare restrictions unreasonable simply based on public policy."

Another example of rules that would be challenged are those which violate the Fair Housing Act Amendments. We provide detail on the Fair Housing Act in another chapter of this book; however, we mention it here as it affects the enforceability of rules and regulations.

"It applies to any real property and it modifies to a large degree a number of recorded restrictions in declarations and master deeds that were recorded prior to the Fair Housing Act Amendments being in place," said Makower. For example, there are many old documents that tried to define a single-family. There are a number of principles that come out of that act that provide reasonable accommodations for the disabled. "You have, in this state at least, the codification of such provisions in the Michigan Condominium Act." You also have a Civil Rights Act in Michigan, The Elliott-Larsen Civil Rights Act, which piggy backs on what the Federal Government has done with the Fair Housing Act amendments.

"Pretty much anything you do in a community association regarding enforcement has potential implications of discrimination, at least, in a civil rights setting. So it is something that all boards must be cognizant of and must consider in making enforcement decisions and passing on requests for modifications and alterations," said Makower.

He explained that these types of complaints are becoming plentiful, and they are easy to file. They are expensive for an association to deal with and ultimately eat away at some of the restrictions you see in the documents. "Allowing pets is another classic restriction now that's being eaten away by Fair Housing Act amendments. Claiming the right to an emotional support pet is a biggie," he said. Pet restrictions have been all but done away with as all the resident needs to do is go to a doctor willing to write a letter stating the resident has some type of issue that is remedied by them keeping a pet.

"The actual legal requirement is a lot more than that, with a lot more specificity, but people are so afraid of being drawn into a civil rights dispute that they let residents get away with things that maybe they shouldn't get away with," he said.

Because of the justifiable fear of facing a civil rights lawsuit, many of these decisions are determined administratively by the associations rather than in a court of law. Thus, the complainant has a good chance of getting their way in these matters.

Appeals to Committees and the Board

Is a committee's decision final when penalizing a resident rule-breaker, or can a resident appeal to an association's board?

"That depends totally upon the governing documents and the action that establishes the committee," said Makower.

He explained that most committees are formed by and staffed by the board of directors. "There are situations where committees are actually specified in the governing documents. Those are called committees of the membership, which means they are committees whose members are elected by the members of the organization and not appointed by members of the board of directors." Committees of the membership have separate powers and are more autonomous from the board of directors than traditional committees (the social committee, communications committee, etc.).

Committees that operate by and through the board of directors usually do not have independent power, other than to recommend to the board. On the other hand, committees of the membership can have separate powers and would not need a grant of authority from the board since they derive their authority from the documents themselves.

However, if a decision has been made by the board rendering a resident guilty of breaking a certain rule, it doesn't make sense for the resident to go to the same committee to appeal. "I've seen plenty of situations where a fine is levied by the board and an appeal is made to the board. Well, what is the purpose of that?" asked Makower. He noted that if an association is going to have an appeal procedure, they should have one that makes rational sense. But appeal procedures before the same people within an organization really don't make sense, and ultimately, if the board makes a decision that a resident disagrees with, the resident should take their appeal to a court of law.

Fines

How does an association determine fine amounts? "In many cases you will find fine amounts or a fine schedule in the documents. It's fairly common in the State of Michigan to have a fine schedule where the first violation gets a notice, the second one gets a fine, the third one gets a fine, the fourth and subsequent ones get a fine, and it's all stated in the documents as to what it is. The beauty of that type of system is it's easy to administer and it takes all the discretion out of the process," said Makower. Once you take discretion out of the process, you remove the possibility of someone saying the board has behaved in an arbitrary or capricious manner.

However, it is not necessary to have a fine schedule, and you can have a system where each fine is determined by the body that is doing the hearing and then ultimately confirmed by the board of directors. Some associations have different fines based on different levels of violations. "I've had associations that deem a leasing violation as more serious than a pet violation or a 'you put your garbage out at the wrong time' violation," he said.

The more discretion you put into the system, the more you need to keep good records of the circumstances that comprise a violation and the fine levied, along with the factual circumstances surrounding that. "If you come up with a similar factual circumstance and do something different at a later date, you're going to find yourself, at least potentially, accused of arbitrary and capricious or discriminatory conduct," said Makower.

"The key is, it's got to be predictable, it's got to be uniform, it cannot be arbitrary, and that's why stated fine schedules generally work better than those that are left to the discretion of the fining body," he said.

Makower also added that associations are not required to provide an appeal process for fines.

What is Due Process?

Due Process has been in US Constitutional laws since the drafting of the Constitution. "You shall not deprive any person of property without due process. Due process, in the condominium or association sense, largely is encountered in the area of non-judicial penal schemes. In most cases, that means fining procedures. Can you issue fines and enforce those fines as your own judge and jury without due process? The answer is no," said Makower.

Due process requires that the person who is being accused is given knowledge of that which they are being accused. There is a certain amount of specificity needed to inform the person of what they did, and when, and that it was in violation of a particularly identified restriction.

"Only when you have adequately apprised somebody of what they're being accused of have you followed due process. Then you go onto the next step in the procedure, which is before you can levy a fine or a penalty against somebody for such violation, they are entitled to a hearing to offer evidence in defense of any allegation that they have violated the provision. So the necessity for a hearing is part of due process," Makower said.

After that, it can be determined that a violation has actually occurred, and the association can fine somebody, since at that point they have afforded the resident due process.

Transparency and Notice in Enforcing and Amending Rules

What is the process for an association to amend their CC&Rs? In a condominium situation, according to Makower, that is covered by the statute that is mandatory and requires two-thirds of all eligible voting co-owners in an association to approve it. In seven different instances noted in Michigan's statutes, mortgagees also need to approve.

How does the governing body make knowledge of its actions available to residents, and what is meant by transparency? Some people who talk about transparency are talking about government by the whole. To them, transparency means everything gets voted on by the members, and the vast majority must agree on everything that is enacted. According to Makower, that is not the practical definition of transparency. The members of association vote for people to serve on the board to make decisions for them.

In its real sense, transparency is where decisions are made known to the co-owners. "Should you open your board meetings so people know what you're doing? Yes," said Makower, "if you can! One problem is some associations do not have a clubhouse or facility for open meetings and you cannot expect board members to open their homes to everyone — it would be another deterrent to serving." However, he said that if those who come to the meetings make those meetings unproductive because they try to insert themselves into the work of the board, that doesn't work. "Many times the problem when you talk about transparency is the question, 'Am I operating an association or am I operating a kibbutz, where everybody has a voice?'" he asked. You can't operate as a kibbutz, otherwise the board will be stymied. There are many tough decisions that need to be made, such as whether or not to raise assessments, and therefore an elected board is needed to make those decisions.

Should there be secret meetings, where there are no minutes kept and no one knows about the meetings?

No, there should not be. But can the board operate without being in full view of the association members, especially when they're deliberating decisions involving a legal privilege or privacy?

"Yes, they should be able to do that," said Makower. "That is not a lack of transparency; that is how you get the job done." There needs to be respect for those volunteering their time as board members to do the job they're elected to do. However, there should be access to records. According to Makower, in the State of Michigan the Condominium Act covers access to records, but meetings and deliberations do not have to be an entirely open process.

What kind of notice is required to inform residents that a new rule is in effect? According to Makower, there is nothing in the law that requires specific notice. You either have no requirement or some stated requirement. The standard in the State of Michigan is a thirty-day advance notice. In some older documents, Makower noted, he has seen provisions for new rules to go into effect in three years.

He also said that you won't see terms of notice in any declaration. It is part of the policy-making of the association to determine how much notice will be given.

Alternative Dispute Resolution

Alternative Dispute Resolution (ADR) is basically arbitration or mediation either inside the association or by an outside party. There could be a number of dispute outcomes that could be imagined as possibilities within an association. "A large enough and active enough association could have public forums to help with sorting out that type of thing, but the bottom line is dispute resolution is largely related to dealing with claims of people that others are violating the documents," said Makower. It could be used where co-owners are complaining about co-owners, the association is complaining about co-owners, or co-owners complaining about the association.

The nature of mediation, which is to get people to talk about and solve their own disputes, in the traditional model, does not require independent knowledge of the underlying subject matter. "I agree with that," said Makower. "To mediate, you don't necessarily need underlying knowledge of the subject matter because mediation is an attempt to get two parties to agree upon a resolution that may or may not be governed by the laws of the community or laws of the state in which it takes place."

On the other hand, arbitration requires knowledge of the subject matter. "So in an arbitration situation you can go ahead and arbitrate before somebody that knows nothing about community associations, as you do when you litigate in front of judges," he continues, "but you are then trusting your ability to educate them to a level that they can make a decent decision." Unlike in a court situation, where you can't choose the judge, in arbitration, Makower explained, you can choose your own arbitrator. You have the best opportunity here to choose someone who is qualified.

Makower recommends that the arbitrator you choose should have knowledge of community association law and governance.

There are no actual decisions imposed by mediators. A mediator does not make decisions. A mediator facilitates discussion, and a resolution that is binding is entered into as a contract between the two disputing parties. This is not the case in arbitration. "An arbitrator makes a binding decision based upon what the contract of arbitration requires," said Makower. "If you arbitrate or agree to arbitrate, Michigan now has adopted the Uniform Arbitration Act. So, unless your agreement to arbitrate has a specific paragraph that you can appeal an arbitrator's decision, arbitrator's decisions are generally final and enforceable by a circuit court," he said.

Who pays for the dispute resolution? Makower said that many modern documents specify that the association may send parties into mediation at the co-owner's expense. If it's an association arbitration, it's probably going to be at least a shared expense between the people agreeing to arbitrate. "And sometimes the association bears the whole expense," he said.

• • •

Some Specific Questions Regarding CC&Rs

Q: Can associations place restrictions that would affect the sale of property in their communities?

"Arguably every restriction placed on properties affects the sale of property, or it affects the value of properties," said Makower. The argument is whether that effect is a positive or negative one. "Arguably, at its base, real property restrictions are upheld and favored by public policy because of a judicial perception that they serve to protect the value of property. All court decisions related to the enforceability of real property covenants are based on the premise that restrictions are desired by those who look at them and then decide to buy property within that particular restricted community," he said.

Restrictions provide the stability of maintaining things that residents don't want changed. The premise of the entire restrictive property scheme is that the rules are desired by the people who will buy the property and are designed to uphold a certain desired community standard. Given this premise, Makower explained, it's difficult to argue that the restriction actually hurts the value of the property.

Classic examples of restrictions that could come into question here would be pet policies and leasing restrictions. Makower stated, "Arguably if you don't allow pets, you restrict the number of people somebody could sell to. Very arguably, if you restrict leasing, you're going to restrict the favorable impression an investor would have looking at property within that particular restricted community."

However, do either of these things devalue the property or increase the value of the property?

"The answer to that depends on who is making the claim," he said. Certainly these types of restrictions limit the number of people who may buy in a particular community. But those who do buy do so knowing about and even desiring the restriction. So then it represents a value. For example, someone purchasing in a community that restricts leasing may desire that community because all the units are owner-occupied. Another example is a buyer who doesn't want to deal with a neighbor's barking dog — a community's no pet policy would be a plus to that buyer.

"Every time you look at one of these 'can this devalue my property' restrictions, when you filter it through the basic, bottom-line justification for property restrictions, the people want it, and therefore it has value even though, arguably, it could devalue to some the desirability of that property," he said.

Q: What are architectural controls, and what is considered reasonable?

Architectural controls are those with respect to the maintenance or construction of exterior improvements of the community. They address any new construction or any reconstruction or updates, alterations or modifications to exteriors of buildings.

What is reasonable is largely what is written in the original documents or amended in the original documents in accordance with the requirements of the particular document. "Obviously the Condominium Act, in cases of restrictions that are amended in bylaws and declarations, has its own stated amendment requirements that are not covered by statute in non-condominium situations in the state of Michigan," said Makower. He explained that you can write anything as a developer's attorney regarding those restrictions, as long as you don't violate any other legal concepts. "For example," he said, "specifying only one entity could construct buildings, unless it's the developer or the declarant, would not be viewed as reasonable."

Pretty much any type of architectural control that doesn't violate other laws will be considered reasonable since the restriction is being placed upon the property prior to it being purchased. Thus, the buyer has knowledge of the restriction prior to the purchase of the property. "Generally architectural restrictions are universally upheld due to their preexisting nature," said Makower, "People know presumably what they're buying."

Q: Can associations require that renovation work be permitted and contractors need to be licensed and insured?

Associations can require contractors to be licensed and insured. However, Makower points out, "Individuals have the ability to pull homeowner's permits and do their own alterations and modifications. You cannot prevent that." You can't have a provision that prevents a homeowner from pulling their own permits and doing the modifications when the city allows it. "That would be one of those situations where the restriction would be declared unreasonable," he said. "You simply have to recognize a homeowner's right to do their own work."

Q: Are play-sets a temporary structure?

According to Makower, in most cases, yes. "There are situations where they can be viewed as being non-temporary, such as when they are built-in or have become a fixture of a residence," he said. In those cases, where they have a permanent foundation, they could be considered non-temporary.

Q: Can associations restrict or prohibit the installation of energy efficient systems for aesthetic reasons?

"Right now, at least in the State of Michigan, yes, you can," Makower said. "It'll probably go the way of satellite dishes — at some point there will be some government intervention which dictates that as a matter of public policy, associations will not be able to restrict certain energy efficient installations for aesthetic or any other reasons, provided they're installed properly and in accordance with any applicable codes and requirements," he said. There are still associations doing that and also amending their documents to restrict solar energy panels on roofs for aesthetic reasons. "Until there's government intervention either by legislation or administrative rule, it is something you can do," he said.

Q: Can an association grant a variance?

Under certain limited conditions, if the association's documents allow it, they can grant a variance. "In order to grant a variance, the very same considerations that apply to municipalities granting variances to their zoning ordinances or building restrictions would be in play. You truly can't grant a variance based on favoritism. You have to grant a variance based on objective standards," said Makower. Those objective standards must include, at a minimum, that the reason for the variance is not self-created by the person requesting that variance. If it is, granting the variance would be an arbitrary or capricious act and therefore could be deemed unenforceable in a court of law, according to Makower.

Q: What are encroachments in regard to common areas, and how are they dealt with?

An encroachment in a common area is when somebody erects something or takes action in an area that is commonly-owned by the association. According to Makower, in a well-documented community there is usually a self-help provision to take action to reduce encroachment violations. In these situations, you'd send a notice for the violator to remove the encroachment, specifying that if it's not removed it will be taken away by the association's maintenance crew.

In the most severe cases, a resident could have encroached on a common area for such a lengthy period of time that they may say that they now own that area individually by adverse possession. "Once you get to that point," said Makower, "it's going to require a court decision to determine that." Of course, it is difficult to imagine residents could take commonly-owned property and possess it individually. However, Makower noted that in a severe situation, an association may need to get a court judgment. When these issues are long standing, they become more costly because they require litigation to sort out.

Q: Can an association be held responsible in a situation where there was insufficient lighting caused by lighting restrictions?

According to Makower, yes. "Any time an association creates a hazardous condition, they can be held responsible for the consequences of creating a hazardous condition," he said. This statement applies to much more than a lack of lighting. Makower explained that in some ways, if you don't attempt to do something, you're better off than when you attempt to do something and don't do it well enough. Essentially, if the association is altering the natural state of the environment and does it in a way that creates or exacerbates a hazard, the association will be liable for the situation they have created. "If you are trying to design or install site lighting for security purposes, you're strongly urged to contact professionals in that industry to give you a professional evaluation of what is required. Follow that professional evaluation to a T, and then you are insulated from liability," he said. If the association decides where light is needed on its own, and then creates an area that in unprotected in comparison to areas they are protecting, the association has then created a hazard. Any time an association is creating modifications for safety they should get an expert's opinion, and follow it. This minimizes any potential liability.

Q: Can associations issue speeding tickets?

"Not in the municipal sense," said Makower. Associations don't have police power in the traditional sense. Instead, they can impose fines or penalties through their fining power for what essentially are violations of the condominium documents of which the rules and regulations are a part. "So if you have a speed limit established by your rules," he said, "and you've posted that speed limit on your streets and everybody is aware of that, you can issue fines to owners who violate those speed limits." The difficulty you run into, he noted, is giving tickets to people who are not co-owners. "Your ability to issue fines is limited to co-owners of the community that you have jurisdiction over," he said. For guests or invitees who speed, you would need to issue the fine to the co-owner they are visiting. Ticketing those guests directly can only be done by a police officer.

Q: What are considered reasonable restrictions on resident's holiday displays?

Makower stressed that when putting together restrictions and rules on holiday displays, associations need to be holiday neutral. "The old days of saying you can display Christmas lights between Thanksgiving and 30 days after the Christmas holiday would not be appropriate," said Makower. He noted that you can't choose certain holidays to name in the rules. You need to have rules for what would be allowed for any holiday. "That doesn't mean that you necessarily get rid of periods of time differentials between different types of holidays," he said.

Holidays that happen in locations with heavy winters can be treated differently than holidays in mild weather. "It's okay to say you have to put up and take down decorations within two weeks of a holiday, except if there are weather conditions that prevent that. You can have it extended to a period of time for when the weather breaks and would allow reasonable access to the outdoors. Again, as long as you're not holiday-specific, you would be fine," he said.

Q: What are the issues with banning political signs?

According to Makower, there are certain types of signage that are going to be a little more problematic than others. However, the bottom line is that in a private community such as a condominium situation, where there is commonly-owned property, associations have the right to restrict. Alternatively, in individually-owned property, such as in HOAs — that will become significantly more difficult because there are court decisions out there that do not even allow municipalities to tell somebody they can't have a political sign on their front lawn. "If a municipality can't do it, then as an association or an HOA you probably can't do it either," he said. "The bottom line is that HOA property is individually-owned property, and there's a certain amount of free speech you're going to have to put up with," he said.

2

Collection of Delinquent Dues

Delinquent homeowner dues accounts can affect a community in a variety of negative ways. Obviously, the association needs homeowner dues to be paid, preferably on time, in order to operate. However there are many residual undesirable consequences of having too many delinquent accounts. A community with an abundance of homeowners in arrears on their assessments could be declined for a capital improvement loan when needed — therefore preventing the community from performing necessary major repairs or replacements. Also, the FHA looks at the number of delinquent homeowners in a community in its approval process, and won't approve communities with over a certain percentage of past-due accounts. If an association can't obtain FHA approval, allowing potential purchasers to obtain FHA mortgages for homes in the community, it can have a huge negative impact on home sales for the entire neighborhood. Cleaning up past-due accounts in an expeditious manner will not only benefit the association itself, but also all the homeowners who have a stake in the community. So how should this be done?

Steps and Options for Collecting Delinquent Dues

There are many ways to deal with delinquent homeowner assessment accounts, and various factors that need to be considered prior to taking any collection action. "The first step is to determine the facts on the account before you and figure out which method of collection is likely to be the most successful given the association's goals," said Michigan attorney Mark Makower.

The process begins by performing a preliminary asset search to determine whether or not the account in question is likely to be collectible. "If they're likely to be collectible, we tend to favor options which result in a judgment — a money judgment for the association. Then we proceed to collect the money that's due," he said.

Makower said that if there is a doubtfulness of collection, associations generally go down a route toward foreclosure. Whether to go about foreclosure by advertisement or by judicial means will depend on various factors. These factors include whether or not there are potential title issues involved. Additional factors are issues involving other encumbrances and liens, as well as priority issues. "The more of those that you see, the more we probably tend to favor judicial foreclosure so we can work out all of those problems at once," he said.

• • •

Two Possible Roads — The Two Forms of Foreclosure

There are two forms of foreclosure that can be pursued with respect to a community association lien provided "power of sale" language is contained in the condominium documents – which most of the times is the case. The following excerpts from a Client Advisory issued by Makower's firm, Makower Abbate, PLLC, provide descriptions of the two.

> **Foreclosure By Advertisement:** The first version that is possible is foreclosure by advertisement. This is entirely a statutory proceeding and is performed in accordance with the provisions of the mortgage foreclosure by advertisement statute. In this type of situation a notice of foreclosure sale is published in the legal news for four weeks prior to the

scheduling of a sale date. That notice must also be posted by the local sheriff or court officer in a number of different public places as well as on the door of the property being sold. It is incumbent upon the party foreclosing to make sure that they have identified and notified all parties with an interest in the property. After the publication period, the sale is then held and it proceeds in the same fashion as outlined below for a judicial foreclosure. Assuming the association ends up with title to the unit for failure of anybody else to bid, the deed is subject to a six month redemption period similar to a judicial foreclosure – after which time the association can proceed to evict the occupant of the unit and either sell the unit or surrender the same to a party with a higher priority.

The major differences between a foreclosure by advertisement and a judicial foreclosure described below is the fact that there is no court proceeding required at the beginning of the process before the sale is held as would be the case in a judicial foreclosure. Therefore, the cost of the judicial proceeding and the time involved (usually about three months) is saved. Unfortunately, unlike a judicial foreclosure, a foreclosure by advertisement can be attacked judicially at any time prior to the expiration of the redemption period. This would involve the filing of a complaint by a party with an interest in the property, claiming that the foreclosure sale should be set aside for any number of reasons related to failure of notice, imperfections in the posting and advertisement of the unit, or even counterclaims involving the assessments on which the foreclosure was promised. If such an action is filed just prior to the expiration of the redemption period, it has the effect of staying the expiration of the redemption and setting the case back to square one pending the outcome of the judicial challenge which may take several months to over a year. It is because of this possibility that we generally recommend judicial foreclosures since an attack on the foreclosure sale after the fact is not possible in a judicial sale. Also, in the case of a judicial foreclosure, you get a personal judgment against the delinquent co-owner as well. With advertisement, personal judgments must be pursued separately and that can only happen after the sale and only if there is a deficiency.

Judicial Foreclosure: The second option is judicial foreclosure. While this generally takes three to four months longer than a foreclosure by advertisement, and costs more, there is an advantage in this procedure because once the sale is held, it is final as the court that issued the judgment also issues an order confirming the propriety of the sale and its final effect. Therefore, after the expiration of the redemption period, the sale cannot be challenged and the association can then proceed to have the unit vacated and either sell it or surrender it to a superior encumbrance. All other proceedings leading up to the sale are identical. The association must still publish notice of the sale and hold the sale in the same fashion as a foreclosure by advertisement. Again, if somebody else bids, the association is paid but if nobody else bids, the association obtains the deed subject to the redemption period.

The procedures leading up to the actual foreclosure sale are different in that the association commences a judicial foreclosure through the filing of a complaint with the circuit court. Depending on whether or not the defendant answers, by either a default motion or a summary disposition motion, the association obtains a judgment of foreclosure and also a judgment of personal liability upon the co-owner who owns the unit. Based upon the obtaining of that judgment, the association moves forward with the sale rather than just publishing the notice as in the case of a foreclosure by advertisement. Obviously, one advantage of this type of proceeding is the fact that after the foreclosure is completed, there is no need to obtain a personal judgment against a co-owner who may have vacated the unit (if you need one still) since one was already granted at the time that the judgment for foreclosure was granted. As indicated above, the other major advantage is that the sale cannot be attacked once it is confirmed by the court as being properly held. In this fashion, judicial foreclosures are more final than a *foreclosure by advertisement and not subject to the risk of substantial delay as is the case with foreclosure by advertisement. For all of these reasons, we recommend and pursue in most cases judicial foreclosure actions.*

•••

What's Next

Once the determination of which route to pursue is made, attorneys normally will inform the association and get their approval prior to commencing the process. "The process always starts with a demand letter being sent to the owner of the unit, and any other people that may be liable, seeking collection of the amounts due or some type of arrangement to have those sums brought current," he said. If they do not receive a response to the demand letter, the attorney will then file a lien upon the unit. If a response to the lien is not received, they will move forward on the path determined prior to starting the process.

Does it make sense for associations to go a different route and sell unpaid assessments to a collection agency? "It doesn't cost you anything," said Makower. "Most companies take all their accounts on a contingency basis and rates vary dramatically in that industry." He cautioned that if you are only referring accounts that you are reasonably sure you will never collect, it doesn't cost you anything, so it doesn't hurt. "What is troublesome is those associations that refer accounts to a collection agency when it is the account of a debtor who can pay and chooses not to. In that type of situation the association is throwing money away. Because the account will be collected, and rather than collecting the full amount and all of your costs and fees in collecting it as an association, by giving it to a collection agency, although you don't pay out of pocket, you're only going to recover a percentage of that account when you could have recovered everything," he said.

Another possible option for those seeking to collect delinquent accounts is Small Claims Court. If you have a debt that is collectible, filing in Small Claims Court is an option for boards or association managers to use to pursue the debt. An attorney would not do this on the association's behalf. "Attorneys are not allowed, so it's not an option for us," notes Makower.

What are the proper means of communication with the debtor during the collections process? "We absolutely encourage, every one of our clients, once you turn an account over to us, do not have any contact or communication whatsoever with the debtor co-owner or the debtor co-owner's representatives," he said. The primary reason for this is that once the collection process starts, the costs of collection are charged to the co-owner. Additionally, having only one party speaking ensures accuracy and accountability.

Also, in many cases they would end up settling for less than the full amount due or agreeing to something they should never agree to. There is also the risk of inconsistency in communication with the debtor co-owner. "Eventually at some point in time if you do that, the co-owner's probably going to request that some or all of the charges be rebated because some or all of these actions may have been unnecessary. We request that all contact be through us, and at that point in time we handle everything with the co-owner or the co-owner's representatives."

Are there ways to set up repayment plans with debtors who express an interest in doing so? According to Makower, there are many ways to do this. However, he cautioned not to accept or even ask for payment plans that are unrealistic. "It does you and it does the homeowner no good to agree to a plan that everybody knows no one can keep," he said. He explained that one of the biggest mistakes he sees associations make is setting arbitrary payment plans without looking at individual circumstances. "And one size does not fit all," he said. "If you force somebody to agree to something that eventually they're going to have to breach, you haven't gained much."

He recommended tailoring a plan that makes sense — one which would provide the debtor the ability to make the agreed upon payments. "First and foremost," he continued, "any payment arrangement that you accept has to, at a minimum, make sure that they're not getting further behind. If they're getting further behind, the inevitable will be that the person will not be able to keep the unit. Why delay the inevitable?"

Something additional to note regarding collection tactics: The Fair Debt Collection Practices Act, a piece of federal legislation, governs the collection of debts against consumers. "It has a ton of different requirements," Makower said, "and yes, attorneys collecting debts for association clients are considered debt collectors under that act and must comply with it."

Must associations comply with the Fair Debt Collection Practices Act when setting up any payment plans or pursuing debtors themselves?

"An association collecting its own debts is not subject to the Act, as it is not engaged primarily in debt collection. So, associations have nothing to worry about. It is the attorneys or managers who may have a concern and yes, various provisions of the Act pertain to the form of allowable communications with the Debtor, so they apply whether you are seeking a payment plan or any other form of collection," Makower said.

Makower also recommended not engaging in any practice to attempt to embarrass the delinquent co-owner. "I don't suggest any of those types of activities because on the back side of that," he said, "if you do it improperly or make an error in the debt, you could be facing defamation liability for erroneously reporting that someone hasn't paid a debt," he said.

He pointed out that it doesn't make sense to take this risk since, if someone can't pay, embarrassing them won't make any difference in their ability to do so.

Once a collection case goes to court, there are a number of different actions that can be taken to collect the debt. "In circuit court, you have the ability, under our statute at least, to sue for both foreclosure and a money judgment for a condominium case. So if you want to get both, circuit court is the only way to get it," said Makower. He explained that if you want to foreclose in any situation, unless you're doing it by advertisement, you also need to go to the circuit court because they have sole jurisdiction to do that. District courts — and small claims courts are part of district courts — can only give you judgments for money. You can't foreclose a lien in district court. Rather, you're going to get a judgment for an amount due.

"The problem with that," Makower said, "is it is a snapshot in time, and you're going to get the amount due as of the day you go in to get your judgment. If another installment becomes due the next day, the next month, or two months down the road, you're stuck with going back to court. The judgment will not pick up future amounts that become due. You will have a set amount, as of a set date, and may have the necessity of going back and doing it again." That is the downfall of district courts. The limitation of jurisdiction in district courts is not usually a problem. Since the limit is $25,000, it would be unlikely for an association to allow a co-owner to become so deeply delinquent without taking action.

Another downside of district court is that it produces an unsecured judgment, which means that it's dischargeable in bankruptcy.

"When you have a foreclosure judgment, you have the right to pursue property. When you have a money judgment, you don't," he said.

There are three ways to collect on money judgments — garnishment, levy and execution.

Garnishment is the seizing of money due. Some examples of what can be garnished are loans due the debtor, bank accounts and employers. "You can garnish in any situation where somebody owes your debtor some money," he said.

A levy is a seizure of personal property. "It commands a court officer to go out and seize valuable personal property and dispose of it and pay the proceeds of any transaction over to the creditor after the expenses of the sale are deducted," explained Makower.

An execution is the same as a levy except it is on real property rather than personal property. "It allows you to attach other property holdings of a person other than the unit in question," he said. Makower also noted that execution can indeed include attaching the unit in question, not just other properties.

Who should initiate the process of filing a lien on an owner's unit?

Makower explained that it's not considered an unauthorized practice of law for someone to file their own liens. However, the problem with people who are not attorneys doing that is if they make mistakes — file for unjustified amounts or amounts in the future, or if they don't follow statutes, such as Michigan's, which says you can't put any collection costs on your lien amount — they are going to make their lien attackable in court, and possibly even voidable, in court.

"Worst case scenario," he said, "if you don't know what you're doing, you can be held responsible for slander of title, which carries with it some fairly severe penalties. You're messing with interests in land, and when you mess with interests in land you either know what you're doing, or hire an attorney who knows what they're doing," he said.

At what point in the process is a lien filed?

"That is variable based on an association's desires. Some place liens immediately and some wait until an initial demand is unsuccessful. In situations where a lien is placed immediately, you expend money and raise the payoff amount when you may not have had to do this with someone who responds to a demand. This may be perceived by the association membership as too severe since we find that almost 40% of all accounts are resolved simply through the demand. On the other hand, filing immediately puts you on record earlier, which can make a difference in certain limited priority disputes. Mitigating that approach, however, is the fact that the delay involved is only 5 weeks or so," Makower said.

Decision-Making Along the Road of Collection

There are many different circumstances dictating the best route for collection. Furthermore, during the process, additional factors can alter the direction the process will take. Here are a few scenarios and factors that affect an association's collection actions.

For example, is it advisable to go after delinquent owners who decide to walk away from their properties, particularly those owners who did a strategic default? Makower said that they determine whether or not to pursue a debtor who has abandoned the property after performing an asset report. If the debtors have assets, he said, yes, it is advisable to go after them. "Because you will collect them," he said.

Makower stated that there are two classes of association debtors — those who can't pay, and those who choose not to pay. "In the category of those who can't pay, it doesn't matter what you do to them," he said. Since they cannot pay, there is nothing you can do that will enhance your ability to collect the debt. "Those who choose not to pay, which includes those who would do a strategic give-back, you will collect from," he said.

Another decision to weigh is whether to pursue foreclosures against delinquent owners or whether it is more advisable to allow banks to foreclose and assume the financial obligations. Makower explained that associations and their attorneys would not be able to obtain the necessary information to make that determination in any situation. "Banks don't necessarily foreclose. The loan can be in default; but the bank can take years and still not foreclose. We've seen situations where banks haven't foreclosed after two or three years," he said. Internal bank matters are not something the association would be privy to.

Makower further noted that the association would not know if the bank was receiving a payout of federal mortgage insurance, for example, or if it has otherwise written off that debt so it is no longer carried on its books. "If they're not going to take action, you have no way of knowing that," he said. He recommended that associations proceed with foreclosure even if there is a bank out there not being paid its mortgage payments. "What you do know is every day you don't do something, you continue to lose assessments," he said.

If the bank comes in during the time that the association has already started the foreclosure, the association can always discontinue it. "But you'll never get the time back that you waste waiting for them," he said.

Once the bank starts the process, at least in Michigan, there isn't much point in the association moving forward with their own foreclosure. Not unless there's an error in the process whereby the association has an argument that they're entitled to a better priority than the bank is giving it. "In those situations, yes, you have to make that argument so your priority is as high as it can possibly be and is accurate with the priority that you should have," he said. "Absent mistakes by the bank and them treating you differently than they should treat you, there is going to be almost no reason why you need to involve yourself in a bank foreclosure." The association's priority, he noted, is set by statute, and they're going to receive whatever is left over, if anything, in the order of their priority. "In most cases today, there's nothing left over," he said, "so there is really nothing to protect."

However, aside from when a bank starts its own foreclosure procedure, Makower pointed out that another circumstance where he would stop collection efforts against a co-owner would be if that co-owner's status had changed to the point where the debt had become uncollectible. "Every now and then, there will be a change in circumstance. Somebody can be perfectly collectible when you begin a suit, and subsequently file bankruptcy and become less collectible afterwards," he said. Makower explained that your debt may not survive the bankruptcy. Alternatively, if the bank pays the sum due when it comes in, why continue to pursue

> **What does expiration of redemption mean?**
>
> The period of redemption is set by statute and is the period of time during which a debtor — or other entity with an interest in the property they want to protect — can pay all sums due and retain title to the property.

the co-owner if you've been paid in full? These are examples of when to stop collection efforts. "But there are very limited circumstances in which you'd do that," he said.

Dealing with Banks after Foreclosure

Foreclosed properties can become an eyesore for certain communities. Particularly in HOAs — lawns go un-mowed, weeds grow, paint peels, pipes freeze and cause leaks. How can associations get banks to handle maintenance issues on foreclosed properties?

"You can sue them," said Makower. He also said that some associations have self-help provisions that allow them to do whatever needs to be done maintenance-wise and to bill the unit. When you have that type of provision, he recommended sending one letter stating the repair or maintenance needs to be done in a specified number of days, and if the work is not done, the association should just proceed with the work and bill the unit. "You're in first position on that unit moving forward, there's no more mortgage, you're going to collect your money from that unit. Don't wait around for the bank to do the right thing. Do it yourself," he said.

There are also limits on the amount of past-due assessments lenders are required to pay. "We don't have a priority lien law in the State of Michigan. But our Condominium Act does indicate that assessments are due from the date of taking title, as opposed to possession. So because of that, and because title in some fashion — equitable title — is obtained by a bank immediately upon the foreclosure sale, not upon expiration of redemption, we are almost always successful in getting the association six months worth of dues from the date of the foreclosure sale forward," said Makower. Anything prior to the date of the sale itself, he noted, cannot be recovered legally in the State of Michigan. "Although, every now and then certain banks will pay it," he said.

Renting a Foreclosed Unit to Recoup Costs

What are the pros and cons of foreclosing on a delinquent unit with the intent to rent the unit to recoup the association's fees?

Makower said that this is often an option where you are not otherwise going to collect and somebody has a higher priority on the Unit that you do not wish to pay or that you believe exceeds its value. And in that case Makower does not see a downside of renting the unit.

"The pros are that you're receiving income toward the unpaid debt and slowly retiring it rather than continuing to receive absolutely nothing from a unit that remains either occupied by someone who's not paying, or totally vacant. So it makes all the sense in the world to rent a unit after foreclosure," he said. He noted that this is especially true if there is a bank out there in the wings that has a mortgage that legally has a higher priority than the association. The one thing to be cautious of here is that you do need to act properly and professionally in your actions as a landlord. The association is advised to hire a professional to handle the landlord responsibilities.

"Make sure that you know what you're doing, and follow all required regulations and laws in your state concerning the rental of real property," said Makower. He noted that condominium association boards are not usually professionals in handling real estate or even homeowner associations for that matter. That's why they hire managers. "I would tell associations who are not familiar with the landlord business, make sure your manager is, or hire somebody who is, so proper disclosures can be given, all procedures for move-in/move-out can be followed, security deposit is properly held and properly refunded and all other requirements of state law are met," he said. He further stressed that since real estate is a regulated industry, you need someone who knows what they're doing.

If a lender does come in when you are renting such a unit, could they argue that there are no delinquent assessments they're required to pay?

Makower explained that there are two types of association documents out there. There are those that have a specified manner in which payments are applied, and those that do not. If you have a provision that says that any money is applied to costs, expenses, and then assessments in the order of its delinquency, and you're renting the unit as an association, you're going to apply the money in the manner which that provision requires. This means that technically, even though you have rental income, that rental income may not be paying current assessments because there are still amounts to be paid from prior due assessments. "So you can very easily in those situations take your rental income, apply it as your documents require, and say to the bank who happens to foreclose in the interim, that there are still unpaid assessments, and they happen to be current assessments that apply to a period of time after which you had a foreclosure sale," he said.

Unless the bank has a receiver, they will not be able to take your rent income. On the other hand, in cases where there is no application of payment language in the association documents, in Makower's opinion, the association would need to pay the current assessment and then apply the rest to the back assessments that may be owed. In that situation, there wouldn't be anything for the bank to pay.

3

The Association's Records

Knowing which records should be kept, where to keep them and how to store them can help an association maintain access to important historical data about itself. Association records should contain information that the board can use as a reference for future projects, or possible evidence in a lawsuit or audit. Records are useful when the board is negotiating contracts for landscaping or snow removal. Boards can refer to work records, financial records or even minutes from the meeting where the contractor was chosen to weigh future decisions.

What to Keep and Where to Keep it

First, you need to determine what types of records need to be kept. This includes a number of different records used in the normal course of an association's operation, such as:

- financial records
- tax records
- unit files or lot files
- work records *(including contracts with vendors, employee records, warranty documents, work logs, etc.)*

Next, you need to determine for how long to keep each type of record. "The type of record determines the length of time for which you're going to need to keep it," said Makower. Corporate records, according to Makower, need to be held basically forever. These include:

- governing documents
- records of elected directors
- meeting minutes *(from both board and association meetings)*

According to Makower, Michigan doesn't mandate a given level of record retention by law. Record keeping mostly has to do with what the governing documents require. For example, some bylaws require that minutes be kept and other bylaws don't mention minutes at all. Always consult your governing documents for specific instructions.

The fact is, Makower said, "You can't prove what you did if you don't keep minutes and records." So it is in an association's best interest to keep accurate and thorough records.

How detailed do board meeting minutes need to be? "Meeting minutes of any kind need to reflect the actions actually taken," said Makower. That is what a proper set of minutes does. Some minutes note every person who had a question and every discussion that took place. "None of that is required for a set of minutes," Makower said. When compiling your meeting minutes, list only what the board specifically resolves to do at the meeting — in other words, the specific motions or actions taken. "They should be less detailed rather than more detailed," he said.

Are there any requirements as to what form records are kept in? More and more people are keeping documents in an electronic format. "That's fine," said Makower, "as long as they're backed-up somewhere and there is more than one copy." He said there is no statute in the State of Michigan on record keeping or how long you need to keep records.

Where may the association records be stored? Can they be stored in the home of a board member? "Well, sometimes that's all you have," said Makower. Sometimes management companies store the records, sometimes they're stored electronically, and sometimes they're stored off-site — sometimes in the Cloud. "There are a number of different ways and places to actually keep your records," he said. There is no particular method of storage that is specified in any statute.

Are there any restrictions on putting records online? According to Makower, there are privacy restrictions that relate to personal information. The same things that can get you into trouble with defamation can get you in trouble for making them public on a website. "You need to make sure certain information is not disseminated in a public manner," he said.

For How Long Do We Need to Keep Records?

Certain documents have requirements outside association provisions that need to be met. "For instance, tax returns and anything that you put in your tax return. If you're able to be audited for seven years, it's best that you keep that information for seven years in case you're actually audited," said Makower.

Your permanent corporate records are the only things you're mandated to keep forever, and that you should keep forever, because they are your corporate history. "Most other documents have a shelf life of some time," he said.

Access to Association Records

Who has access to records? According to Makower, only members of the organization and their advisors have access to records. The association is entitled to put a process in place for fulfilling residents' requests to view association records. However, Makower noted that it needs to be a reasonable process. "Can they make it an onerous situation when you have a statutory right? Arguably you can't because you have a statutory right," he said. You can't do something such as requesting payment in order to see the records.

However, Makower said that if a resident requests copies of documents, and the association incurs expenses making those copies, it would be reasonable to ask for reimbursement for those expenses. You can also specify that a resident can only come in for a single day every two weeks, as an example, because they would otherwise disturb the operation of the association. This would be reasonable.

Even still, some records need to remain private, or at least until a court order says they're no longer private. "Certain records have legal privileges attached to them, like communications from an attorney. Certain records have liability attached to them if you disseminate them, like potential breach of privacy issues and defamation issues," he said. You need to keep certain information private, such as:

- account balances
- Social Security numbers
- other sensitive, personal information

4

Association Board Member Elections

Cultivating, nominating and electing board members is something that should always be on the minds of current board members. Politics in any arena can be tricky, but in associations it can also sometimes be difficult to find people willing to serve. Many people feel unqualified or even afraid to volunteer due to fears of being taunted by potential disgruntled residents. While these fears are not wholly unfounded, current board members should encourage volunteerism by running fair elections, showing that residents with different types of views and knowledge are needed and desired, and letting potential candidates know their service will be valued, even if all residents don't agree with every decision they make. Most associations have safeguards in place indemnifying board members from potential liability, so if a resident has the time and desire to serve, they shouldn't be afraid to run for the board.

Election Procedures

There is no statutory requirement for associations to have written election procedures. Makower pointed out that in Michigan, since these associations are mainly nonprofit corporations, if you don't have election procedures in your documents (which is rare), you will find enough in the Nonprofit Corporation Act to have an election.

Is there a legal obligation to provide notice of an election? Makower noted that every single governing document requires a notification of a meeting for an election, or a meeting of any kind. There are also timeframes specified for this notice. "Under our Nonprofit Corporation Act, it's at least ten days and not more than sixty days," he said.

The frequency of these elections depends on the circumstances of each association. However, Makower said that in Michigan, associations are required to have an annual meeting of the membership of an association. "Whether or not they have to elect people at that meeting depends on whether there are any open positions," he said. It is stated in the governing documents when an association's annual meeting should take place each year and whether the change in board members should be staggered. "These are all matters that are controlled by the governing documents."

Can an association install term limits for board members? "Sure," said Makower, "but should they? No way." Makower pointed out the fact that term limits basically limit the talent pool stepping up to the board. These are volunteers who offer their time to the association, and not everyone is willing to serve. So if you term-limit those willing to serve, who will succeed these willing co-owners?

In an election, those being voted into positions are directors of the board. Note the distinction between directors and officers:

Directors: When you're talking about nonprofit corporations, which most associations are, directors are generally elected by members of the association. They are vested with the power and authority to direct the corporate affairs of the association.

Officers: Officers are generally appointed by the board of directors, and they have jobs to do, but they don't have a vote at the board meetings. In most cases officers are directors as well, but legally they have different rights and responsibilities depending on whether they are acting as directors or officers.

Nominations

When in pursuit of new board members, how is the nominating committee chosen? Many documents specifically indicate what the composition of the nominating committee will be, and in other documents there is no direction whatsoever. There is no requirement in Michigan to have a nominating committee. "Again, in most cases a nominating committee is not going to be a committee of the membership. It's going to be a committee appointed by the board and therefore there will be some provisions in the documents saying who has to be or may be on the nominating committee. Beyond that, the board will have the discretion as to who they choose for the nominating committee," said Makower.

Are nominations from the floor allowed? In many cases you'll have a nominating committee but you'll still also allow nominations from the floor or nominations by self-submittal. "In those cases it's fairly easy for an individual to nominate him or herself, or have one of their friends nominate them," he said. However, some associations have provisions in their documents that call for a closed slate prior to the time of the meeting and no nominating at the meeting. "If you're not nominated, and you haven't submitted your nomination by other means that are allowed prior to whatever the deadline date is, you simply are not going to be allowed to run," he said. Basically, this issue is document-specific.

Can an association board endorse a slate of candidates or a single candidate? "Sure, and it often happens," says Makower. He said that doing this carries some implications. "If you have a highly popular board that endorses a candidate it will ensure that candidate gets elected. If you have an unpopular board and you endorse a candidate, you'll probably ensure they don't get elected," he pointed out.

Can an association adopt a rule that restricts people from becoming board members? "Yes," Makower said, "but again, it's discussed throughout these chapters, the regulation must be reasonable. And that primarily means you can't be discriminating against people." What you can do is have a rule that states that someone who has been convicted of a crime that involves dishonesty or lack of integrity in the handling of money can't serve on the board. It becomes a little more questionable when you have an association that wants to adopt a rule, for example, stating that only resident owners and no investor owners can hold a position on the board. "This is unreasonable because you are discriminating against a non-resident owner when non-resident ownership is allowed," he said. And of course, you can't violate any civil rights laws such as stating that only males can serve on the board.

Can an association request a background check on potential board members? Generally in a situation like that I would say no because you have existing board members running checks on other people," he said. There is also the question of what is done with the information obtained in a background check. "The board is not a police force. It owes no duty to the membership to do this. You can end up having liability potentially from defamation or other criminal acts by doing it and handling the information incorrectly, so why would you?" he asked.

Campaigning & Voter Registration

During the campaigning phase of the election, do associations need to provide access to association media for candidates to campaign?

Makower does not recommend allowing campaigning through these resources. "Arguably, if you are allowing somebody to campaign through association resources, you have to allow everybody to do so," he said.

Does an association need to require residents to register in a board election? Most associations do since it needs to be established who the owners of the property are. "Most of these organizations require ownership of property in order to be a member," said Makower.

Ballots, Voting & Tallying

The ballot process depends on the bylaws of a particular association. Directors are usually elected at the annual meeting of the association, and it is noticed ahead of time. "You just follow the election procedures that are given to you at the meeting by the people who are running the meeting," he said.

Generally, the ballot process involves the following:
- announcing candidates
- taking nominations from the floor
- closing nominations
- appointing inspectors

- hearing from the candidates
- voting
- collecting the votes
- having the votes tallied by the inspectors of the election

Makower also explained that ballots are not recorded — meaning they're not in the public record. They are on a tally sheet, and an association can either keep the ballots themselves, or they can destroy them in lieu of the tally sheet. "That's up to the individual corporate practice," he said.

Who has access to election results? "In both nonprofit corporations, which are HOAs and condo associations, the members of the organization have the right to inspect the records of the association under procedures for requesting the same," said Makower. "Upon appropriate request, that would be a record of the association that somebody would be entitled to view."

Proxies

For those unable to attend the election, what is the process of establishing a proxy vote? According to Makower, proxies are either permitted or they're not. The documents may state a limitation on the use of proxies, which is valid if it's contained in the documents. Otherwise proxies are generally available. A proxy needs to have certain legal requirements met. "It has to designate who the vote is being given to, for what it is being allowed to be used, and it has to be given by the person authorized to give away or vote for the unit in question," said Makower.

He also said that proxies can be either general or specific. "Obviously in the case of an open election, where you have nominations from the floor at the time of the meeting, the entire slate isn't known ahead of time. Arguably in such a case, you can only use a general proxy because a person filling out a specific proxy ahead of time wouldn't have any idea of what the total question would be, because you wouldn't know who all the candidates would be," he said. If the vote is for something that can be established ahead of time, such as a vote for an amendment of the documents, a specific proxy can be used, along with instructions on how the unit owner would like the proxy to vote.

Cumulative Voting — What is It?

To illustrate the definition of cumulative voting, Makower gave an example. "You have 3 open positions on the board, and you have 3 candidates for those 3 positions. Everybody has the right to cast 3 votes, one each for the open position. That is normal voting. If you were cumulatively voting, a person would have 3 votes that they could give to the same individual," he said.

Once the voting is complete, it is the role of an election inspector to count and tally the ballots and certify the result. "Usually the volunteers for these roles are from the membership who are neither running for the board nor related to someone that is running for the board," said Makower.

A Tied or Challenged Vote

How should the association proceed if the election results in a tie? Makower suggested, if this happens, you should first ask the parties who are tied if one is willing to withdraw. "If they do, that resolves the problem, if not, you can revote," he said.

What is the process for an election challenge or recount? Makower said that in Michigan, you would probably need to file a lawsuit. "Certainly you can review records and make your own determination of what you think happened, but in the end, to mandate another meeting you're going to need a court order," he said.

5

The Fair Housing Act & Civil Rights

Violations of the Fair Housing Act can result in severe penalties for associations. Being knowledgeable of how to govern your community responsibly in this regard is highly important.

What is a common-sense approach to stay in compliance with the Fair Housing Act? "Treat everybody the same," said Makower. "Review all of your actions through a standard of equal treatment of everyone," he said. The minute you see something which possibly excludes or targets someone in particular, you have reason for looking into what you're doing further, and possibly seeking legal counsel. "If it doesn't apply to everybody, it has the potential to be discrimination," he said.

He explained that problems with the Fair Housing Act can result in some very substantial liability for the association. "Fair Housing Act compliance in the State of Michigan is handled by the Civil Rights Commission. The Civil Rights Commission, at no cost to the complainant, will institute an investigation against the association to determine whether or not a person's rights have been violated. It is best to try to get rid of that as quickly as possible, from the standpoint of the time it takes to go through the process. Eventually, if the process continues, there will be an administrative hearing to determine if you have violated the Fair Housing Act and somebody's civil rights. There you are at a distinct disadvantage as an association because you are in front of an administrative agency that has the power to interpret and enforce its own rules," said Makower. He explained that the Civil Rights Commission is basically it's own judge and jury. "You don't necessarily want to put yourself in front of an administrative proceeding arguing that you have not committed discrimination, when the Civil Rights Commission is coming to an administrative hearing after going through an investigation stage and saying yes, there is reason to believe you have," he said.

Additionally, the Fair Housing Act has significant penalties associated with it. "In some of these discrimination cases with animals and restricting facilities to certain classes of people, and that sort of thing, it's not uncommon to see judgments entered in the hundreds of thousands of dollars," he said.

Makower explained that only after going through the administrative hearing are you allowed to appeal the decision in a court of law. "So it can be exceedingly time-consuming and exceedingly expensive," he said.

What are some of the civil rights and how do they apply to associations?

For associations — like any governmental entity, or any private citizen — there are limitations on how they can treat others. Associations, like anybody else, cannot discriminate against any protected class or due to one's:
-gender
-race
-ethnicity
-religion
-sexual orientation

"So associations, especially when you're talking about enforcing restrictions, and applying their own little penal systems, in the form of fining procedures and that sort of thing, must treat everybody the same. The restrictions cannot be discriminatory either in form or in application. Decisions cannot be arbitrary and what they call 'capricious.' So pretty much everything that an association does — in doing its job to enforce restrictions, in doing its job to provide services to the residents of its community, is going to have implications in the civil rights arena," he said.

Any time an association strays from uniformity or equal treatment, they face the possibility that someone will file a civil rights complaint.

Could Fair Housing Act Violations be considered civil violations or criminal penalties? "They are civil. They could rise to the level of being criminal as well. For instance, in the case of taunting, it clearly is a violation of somebody's civil rights and can rise to the level of being considered ethnic intimidation, which is a criminal act and can be punished as a criminal act as well. It is possible that you can have conduct that is both a civil violation and a criminal violation at the same time," he said.

What constitutes problematic wording in a covenant or rule made up by the association? Problematic wording includes any covenant or rule that is not neutral in terms of age, gender, religion, sexual orientation, etc. "The minute you start creating distinctions, you've got a potential problem," said Makower.

"Discrimination, in a legal sense, is all based on whether or not you are doing something to an identifiable protected class," he said. He also explained that over the years the law has evolved in finding and adding protected classes. "Age is a protected class, races are protected classes, genders are protected classes, sexual orientation is now a protected class, recognized religions are protected classes — it's a slowly moving target," he said. He noted that these classes encompass nearly everyone.

Religion in Associations

"From a legal standpoint, is religion a potential legal concern in the area of civil rights? The answer is yes," said Makower. He provided an example that you cannot, in your rule making, favor one religion over another. "A classic example are the associations who have rules and regulations for when you can put up your 'Christmas lights' and must take in your 'Christmas lights,' but never permitted or had a rule dealing with anybody's Halloween decorations, Easter decorations, Kwanza decorations, Hanukah decorations, or other religious or non-religious holidays. You have to be content-neutral in your rules," he said. You cannot favor or oppress any given religion in what you do.

How are religious displays treated in the Fair Housing Act? "If you're giving one religion the opportunity to do something that you're not giving another religion, you're discriminating, and that would be prohibited by the Fair Housing Act or other applicable Civil Rights laws," he said. He explained that there is no law that says that you need to allow people to display holiday decorations or lights of any kind on commonly-owned property. "Many associations choose to allow people to do that. Well, once you venture into the area of doing that, which is discretionary, you need to make sure you do it for everyone," he said.

Can associations prohibit religious services held in common areas? Makower said, yes, as long as they're restricting all religious services, not just certain ones.

Sex Offenders in Associations

Are sex offenders or individuals who pose a direct threat to a community considered disabled? For Fair Housing Act purposes, can there be restrictions against them?

Makower said that, based on the sex offender category, that is not a disability. "Specifically in Michigan, you can have provisions targeted at prohibiting residence in your community by sex offenders," he said.

Rules Regarding Children

Are associations allowed to have any bias against allowing residence by families with children? "The only bias that is tolerated would be with respect to communities that are certified as housing for older people. That is government-sanctioned discrimination against people under the age limit," he said.

For communities with children, how can pool and clubhouse rules discriminate against children, and is it okay for associations to establish rules restricting children from these areas? Makower noted this has become a very changing area due to recent court decisions. "It is very possible for associations to get into trouble on the pool and clubhouse restrictions against children," he said. "Largely because, again, what is the norm in those situations is the picking of some arbitrary age over which you allow people in the pool, under which you either prohibit them or require them to have some type of supervision," he said.

He again stressed that the association's rules need to have some type of rational basis. "Nobody is going to tell you there aren't rational bases for restrictions on toddlers and infants. There are. But they're not across the board because you also have, by the same token, things that you can buy for toddlers and infants that remove the danger that they would otherwise pose to your clean water," he said.

Rules and regulations need to be carefully crafted, keeping in mind objective standards. You can't use generalizations or stereotypes in creating rules. "Why is sixteen the magic age, or twelve, or thirteen? Why not instead focus on whether or not the person has a certificate from a swimming class indicating they can swim?" Focus on the real issue, in this case, the ability to swim, not the age. "That's where you run into problems," he said, "You can't overly generalize. You have to use some objective standard to differentiate."

This doesn't mean you can't restrict certain people or uses of the pool at certain times. For example, when time is set aside during specified hours for adult swim or lap swimming. "It's the stereotypes and generalizations that are going to get you in trouble," Makower said.

Pets and the Fair Housing Act

Is an association required to allow animals for those who have a prescription or note from their doctor for a comfort or service animal? "It's not all that simple, but in essence, these days it comes down to, in almost all cases, if somebody is willing to pursue what is needed to satisfy the Fair Housing guidelines, yes, you're going to have to be permitting pets, regardless," said Makower.

Does an association have any right to question the resident about the prescription or note? "You don't have a right to question somebody about it. What you have a right to do is a right to request that the adequate or required information be contained in the document," he said.

You won't see a statement in the Fair Housing Act that says that, if you have a note from your doctor, you can have a pet. "It's not nearly that simple," said Makower. He noted that the person writing the letter needs to be qualified to do so. "It doesn't mean they have to be a physician, but they do have to have appropriate qualifications. There has to be the identification of disability," he continued. There also needs to be a connection between the disability and the keeping of a pet as part of the treatment plan, or way to ameliorate, to some degree, the effects of the disability. "There is lots of information required and some dots that have to be connected, at least in some arguable fashion, before the letter is going to be an appropriate submission. So if you don't have everything you need," he said, "and that's required by the law, yes, you're entitled to ask for it."

What is the difference between a comfort animal and a service animal? "They're entirely different," said Makower. "Service animals are actually going to have some type of certification training behind them. They can be seeing-eye dogs — that's one type of service animal. There are various others, where they actually assist the person in conducting day-to-day activities of some sort," he said. Alternatively, he explained, comfort animals are usually there for psychological reasons, or they are something that makes a person feel emotionally better.

However, according to Makower, both types of animals are covered by the same set of regulations under the Fair Housing Act. "If you provide the requisite information," he said, "it doesn't matter whether it's a certified service animal or a comfort pet, you're going to have to allow it."

Can associations restrict the size of these animals?

"In the State of Michigan that's going to be exceedingly difficult because we have a couple of cases, decided by the Court of Appeals, that basically determined that a size or weight restriction on animals would be unenforceable because it is 'unreasonable.' And by unreasonable, the judge in the first of those cases determined that the size and weight of an animal itself does not have any logical relationship to the potential harm that was the target of the restriction. And as part of his explanation, he said a forty pound pit bull is going to be far more dangerous to the community as a whole than a ninety-five pound black Labrador," said Makower.

Does the American's with Disabilities Act (ADA) affect how an HOA draws up its own rules on service animals?

Makower's opinion is that it doesn't. "The association is going to find itself implicated not through the ADA, but through the Fair Housing Act," he said. The ADA, he explained, only applies to public accommodations. ADA implications may apply to association facilities that are open to the public, but not within units. The ADA is much more specific with respect to construction standards for making public facilities accessible, but in the area of service animals, there will be nothing more in the ADA than is already required by the Fair Housing Act.

Is it permissible for the association to restrict certain areas where the comfort animals are allowed? Makower said that you can restrict only if there is some health regulation that you need to comply with. "I know it's not even required to keep them out of pool areas," he said. Thus said, there would be a limited amount of places where you could restrict them, if any.

Is it common to require that these animals be photographed when they first come onto a property? "Sure, as long as it applies to any animal," he said. He explained that it's perfectly reasonable for an association to require the registration of pets. "It should not just want and limit itself to the registration of some pets, because if it does, that's going to be an unreasonable restriction," he said. If it's seeking registration and/or pictures of all pets, he notes, there is nothing wrong with that.

Can an association, while allowing comfort animals, limit the number of those animals that a resident has? Makower said, in his opinion, that he believes you can do that. "In most cases, unless there is a demonstrated need for more, and that would come from, obviously, the treating physician, we normally limit to one. In most cases you're pretty much limited to one," he said.

6

Transitions

What is a transition? Makower explained, "In Michigan, in the condominium sense again, the statute talks about the 'transitional control date,' and it is the date on which the management and the administration of the condominium is transferred from a board of directors controlled by the developer to a board of directors controlled by the non-developer owners. A similar scenario happens in an HOA. At some point in time the declarant is no longer the only party who can vote and the only party who administers the association and the declaration, and there's actually a board of directors elected by the non-declarant owners to govern the association. That is considered to be the transition."

What if construction defects or problems are found prior to transition?

In this case, homeowners would hope for the developer to take it upon itself to address those issues. However, Makower explained that in many cases this does not happen. "Before the transition, the vast majority of the board is controlled by the entity that presumably would be responsible. So, while something could and should be done before transition, the fact is that issues are rarely addressed, because the people in charge would basically be looking to impose liability on themselves," said Makower. He explained prior to the transition, in the condominium sense, there is a period of time during which an advisory committee made up of non-developer owners is formed. This committee brings issues to the attention of the developer-run board of directors that are brought to their attention by other non-developer owners.

Is there ever a situation where a developer will pay expenses out of their own pocket to keep assessments artificially low?

Makower said yes, and that this frequently happens. "If after transition the association finds that its assessments have been kept artificially low, or in another sense it finds they overpaid a bunch of expenses or the developer is claiming it made a loan to the association for which it now wants reimbursement, there are a number of legal defenses against a developer doing that. Case law exists nationally indicating that for a developer-controlled board to artificially keep assessments low for the purpose of selling units, is a violation of the fiduciary duty that the board owes to the membership," he said. Associations have the right to pursue that scenario judicially.

Homeowners themselves do not have the right to inspect a developer's financial records. "Absent litigation, you're never going to be able to do that. You don't have any specific rights. You can get the right to look at developer financial transactions once you file a lawsuit through discovery procedures," Makower said.

If the developer enters into a contract on behalf of the association, what happens after transition? In this case, is the association responsible?

"Here in Michigan under the Condominium Act, after the transitional control date, if the developer has contracted with itself or its affiliate for the purposes of managing the association beyond the transitional control date, the association has statutory rights to terminate that arrangement," he said.

As far as other short-term contracts, the terms of termination would actually depend on the contract that has been signed. "If you have long-term agreements, and you can show it's the developer or an affiliate of the developer, you can cancel that portion beyond one year according to our statute as well."

7

Construction Defects

What is a construction defect and what should an association do if they discover they have one? A construction defect is a condition existing due to an error made during construction. For an association to remedy the defects while still pursuing damages from the developer, Michigan attorney Mark Makower recommended proceeding with the repairs and documenting the conditions. "The bottom line is because the developer may be responsible for a problem does not exempt the association from its obligations and duties under the recorded documents. So if this is a common element for which the association is responsible, and it's defective, it may take two to five years to sue the developer for correction of that defect. The association cannot ignore the problem for that long and indeed has an obligation to make sure the damage does not get worse. So, once you put the developer on notice that there's a problem and needs to fix it, if he doesn't, the association really has an obligation to move forward to take care of those things for which it's found responsibility," he said.

He urged that the contractors doing the work document everything they see through photographic evidence, which you should preserve for a later time. "You have the added ammunition, rather than relying on estimates at the time you pursued the claim, you have actual costs and expenses, and a pictorial history of exactly what was wrong and how it was fixed," he said. Proper evidence of the defect is very important. "Liability is the biggest thing and there is no liability without evidence."

For any individual owners in an HOA, those owners would need to pursue any defects within the confines of their own property themselves.

Makower also noted that prior to pursuing any defect litigation, you need to obtain an evaluation from an expert in the field to determine the nature and extent of the defect.

The key is to document everything.

When and how should an association notify a developer of a problem?

According to Makower, the developer needs to be notified of a problem during the time in which the developer is still responsible. "We have as part of the Condominium Act in our state a specified statute of limitations for bringing claims. So during the period that the developer is still subject to the statute of limitations, you certainly are going to make demands upon the developer for everything that you believe and can show is the result of deficiencies in the developer's or its contractor's performance," he said.

Makower stated that you should notify the developer through any form of written communication. "You want to make sure it's written so it's traceable and it can be proven," he said. Again, this underscores the importance of good documentation.

What if a developer claims a warranty has expired?

"They probably will claim a warranty has expired," said Makower, "but there are several concurrent warranties that go with the sale of property. In most cases, you have not only expressed warranties, but you have implied warranties." Whether or not these warranties can or cannot be disclaimed would be up to the claimant's attorney to handle.

"Even if you have an expressed warranty that has expired, (those are usually the one-year limited warranty when you buy a home), you have implied warranties of fitness, habitability, and of construction in a workmanlike manner — all of those implied warranties, which if not validly disclaimed, would run for a period of up to six years, as opposed to the one-year, limited warranty that comes with the sale."

A claimant's attorney needs to look at all the potential warranties and applicable provisions as to when the claims accrue (that is when the warranty period begins to run). In Michigan several limitations periods begin to run only when you know of a claim or should have known of a claim. Be aware, as well of any Statutes of Repose that may be applicable.

Arbitration in Construction Defect Claims

According to Makower, the vast majority of judicial contests over construction litigation are eventually referred by the bench to arbitration. "It is their favorite method for trying to resolve construction disputes, primarily because judges don't want to learn all about construction. There is an awful lot of detail and an awful lot of expertise needed. So it is consistently felt in Michigan that it is preferable to have construction cases arbitrated as opposed to actually tried," he said.

However, in Michigan, associations are not required to go into arbitration. "We have a statutory Condominium Act that allows arbitration by consent of the people involved. There is also a statutory provision that mandates arbitration if one or the other person chooses it — in certain situations that are involving claims against the developer, either claims by the co-owners against the developer or claims by the association against the developer. You have the unilateral ability to take certain of those claims and submit them to arbitration under certain dollar levels. For an individual it's $2,500; for an association it's $10,000," he said.

8

Reserve Studies

What are reserves, and why do associations need to have them? In order to answer these questions, and provide other important details on this topic, we spoke with John P. Poehlmann, RS, a principal from the Milwaukee, Wisconsin office of Reserve Advisors, Inc., a company specializing in reserve studies, serving clients in all 50 states and in 35 countries worldwide.

"Reserves are funds that are collected by the association from the homeowners on a monthly, quarterly, or annual basis, and set aside into a reserve account for the purpose of replacing the common elements of the association as they wear out," said Poehlmann. The reserve amounts are most commonly included as part the co-owner's regular association fee. The elements the funds are set aside for include those undertaken as large capital projects, such as roof and siding replacements or pavement replacements. Although it is ideal for associations to have sufficient reserves for items such as these as they are needed, that is not always possible. In instances where reserves fall short, associations are faced with three undesirable options: 1) impose a special assessment on the co-owners; 2) borrow funds for the capital project from a bank, or 3) postpone projects.

How Much Should Be Held in Reserves?

Of course, it would be impossible for anyone to randomly decide the proper amount to hold aside in reserves. Many factors must be examined, including the age and condition assessment of all the common elements the community association is responsible for, maintenance practices, interest earned on the reserve funds, as well as adjusting for inflation to the time each of those would need to be repaired or replaced. This is where a professional reserve study comes in. Often conducted by engineers, reserve studies offer a detailed analysis of all of these factors, and provide amounts the association can depend on for ensuring adequate reserves will be there when the association needs them.

Reserve studies have evolved over the years to where they are available in various forms of sophistication, ranging from simplistic forecasts with limited support to comprehensive studies that provide advice that can save associations money. Today one can obtain a professional reserve study that contains cloud-based software that enables boards and managers to have a dynamic, "living" reserve study, that they can easily update as each actual capital project is completed and conduct unlimited "what if" scenarios.

Preliminary Work for the Reserve Professional

Prior to starting the reserve study, the association should provide the reserve professional with copies of the community's governing documents — the declaration, bylaws, CC&Rs, and any other legal instruments that identify what the association is responsible for. "These documents will identify the property components for which the association is responsible for maintaining," said Poehlmann.

In addition to examining the documents, Poehlmann recommended convening with association leadership to ensure the actual needs of the community are addressed by the reserve study. "Equally, or even more important, our engineers have a thorough discussion with management and/or board members or committee members about each of the common elements and whether they want it included in the reserve study that we're going to prepare for them," he said.

There are several good reasons why the reserve professional doesn't rely exclusively upon what's in the governing documents. "First and foremost," said Poehlmann, "we're not lawyers and governing documents are legal documents. We use them as a starting point to get a general idea of the size and complexity of the common elements." Also, he said that association documents are often not specific enough to properly determine which common elements are maintained through the association's reserve account. The association board or trustees might treat the maintenance and replacement of certain common elements through the association's operating budget and not the reserve budget. "I'll give you a simple example — mailbox stations. While a mailbox station might be considered a significant item worthy of inclusion in the reserve budget for a small association of ten units, the replacement of mailbox stations might fall under the operating budget as maintenance in an association comprised of hundreds of homes as it's, relatively speaking, a very small item to them," he said.

While the association is responsible for maintaining the common elements, there is latitude for the board to choose how they maintain the elements, and from which budget, reserve or operating, they take funds to repair or replace. So for these reasons, a discussion with association leadership is key.

Performing the Reserve Study

Poehlmann explained that a reserve study is made up of two parts, as defined by Community Associations Institute (CAI) and the Association of Professional Reserve Analysts (APRA) — the physical analysis and the financial analysis of the common elements.

The physical analysis is comprised of three things. First is the component inventory, which is an identification of the common elements and their quantities, such as square feet, square yards, number of street lights, etc. Second, a condition assessment is performed, which is an evaluation of the current condition of each component based on the observation of the engineer performing the reserve study. Last is the life and valuation estimate. This is where the reserve professional's engineering team determines the useful life, the remaining useful life — or better stated, how much longer the component will last before it has to be replaced — and what is the repair or replacement cost of each component.

The financial analysis has two components. First is an analysis of the fund status. This looks at the current amount of money in the association's reserve fund at the time the engineer conducts the reserve study. It will be noted on the study as of a specific date, often the beginning of the fiscal year for the association. "This is a starting point for the engineer as he or she conducts the financial analysis portion of the reserve study," said Poehlmann.

Second is the funding plan. "This is the plan that identifies the unit or homeowners' reserve contributions that go into the reserve account to offset the anticipated future capital expenses and pays for those capital projects as they become necessary," he said. The funding plan extends a minimum of 20 years into the future, and, more commonly, is developed as a 30-year forecast.

The Many Benefits of Having a Reserve Study

Aside from having the information in the reserve study itself, there are other benefits associated with having a professional reserve study performed.

One benefit is that the reserve study can point out potential problems the association doesn't know about. "You'd be surprised how often maintenance issues are overlooked," said Poehlmann. The reserve professional could also find possible unbudgeted or over budgeted items. "We like to look at the entire operating budget, which includes the reserve budget," he said. There are two reasons for doing this. One is to make sure that all property is accounted for and nothing was omitted from both budgets. The second reason is to ensure that no items were double counted and in both budgets. "When that happens, the association is obviously over-assessing," he said.

Another major benefit of a reserve study, when followed by the association, is that it will eliminate, or certainly greatly reduce, the possibility of special assessments. "Picture yourself as part of a young couple who recently bought a condominium trying to make ends meet and getting a surprise special assessment bill in the mail from the association saying that you have to come up with $4,000 in the next six months for a re-roofing project that wasn't planned for," said Poehlmann. Reserve studies make it easier for homeowners to manage their personal long-term financial planning by ensuring stable association fees, with only minimal and predictable increases.

Preservation of the market value of units or homes in the community is another benefit of having and following a proper reserve study. "This is a big one because peoples' single largest investment is usually their home. A reserve study will help maintain the property in good condition, which helps strengthen the market values of the homes," said Poehlmann.

The reserve study provides benefits to the board as well as homeowners. Since one of the board's primary responsibilities is to maintain and protect the common property of the association, a reserve study helps them fulfill that fiduciary duty. The reserve study can also help the board members reduce claims of fiscal mismanagement by homeowners. "And having that long-term plan saves boards countless hours and meetings. The reserve study gives the board that long-term financial master plan that they need to prepare for the short-term and long-term," said Poehlmann.

For the property manager, the reserve study helps prepare the community for capital projects. "They need to know when capital projects are coming down the pike so they can go out to bid and help the board in understanding the bids," said Poehlmann. It's also a great tool when planning the next year's budget. The information in the reserve study will help free up the manager to focus on the many other property management functions.

Reserve Studies and State Requirements

While some states have legal requirements regarding reserve studies, many still don't. "For instance, the State of California requires that associations hire a professional reserve firm to provide a full reserve study with site inspection every three years, and an annual update in the years that a full reserve study was not provided," said Poehlmann. Nevada and Virginia require a professional reserve study every five years. According to Poehlmann, other states that have statutes that involve either funding reserves, establishing reserve accounts, or rules relating specifically to reserve studies include: Minnesota, Michigan, Ohio, Hawaii, Washington, and others. "The key thing that we've found over the years is that the number of states that are enacting legislation is growing. There is clearly a trend toward more legislation, not less," he said.

When Should the Reserve Study Be Done and How Long Does It Take?

Poehlmann recommended that a full reserve study, which includes a site inspection and condition assessment, should be conducted as soon as possible after transition from the developer. "Then it should be updated with a site inspection at least every three years and certainly no later than every five years," he said. Another good time to have an update is after major changes to the property, such as following a large capital project. "However, it is very important for the board and management to review the reserve study every year. Many boards use the study throughout each year," he said.

The initial reserve studies themselves can take anywhere from two weeks to three months upon authorization from the association, depending on several factors. "Weather conditions can slow down the development of a reserve study. We sometimes experience delayed inspections in the Midwest and Northeast due to extended bad weather," said Poehlmann. The engineer needs to be able to see the roofs and pavement in order to assess their conditions, so if there is snow and ice on their surfaces that isn't melting, that would cause a delay. Also, the scheduling time varies for different companies, so associations should ask potential reserve professionals about their time-frames and schedules.

If Followed, Does the Reserve Study Guarantee There Will Be No Special Assessments?

Poehlmann said that the reserve study should be used as a guide for future planning. "No one can predict with complete accuracy when capital replacements will be necessary. Weather conditions, for example, can alter what the reserve study provider projected several years earlier," said Poehlmann. Even so, the reserve study is going to give the association the best chance of properly planning and funding their reserves.

To further insulate the community from the possibility of special assessments or needing a bank loan, Poehlmann recommended the reserve professional consider a cushion when developing the funding plan so there is money available in the event that a capital repair or replacement takes place sooner than initially projected in the reserve study. Another safeguard against the unexpected is to have frequent updates conducted on the reserve study. "The initial study is a snapshot in time, and com-

Funding Strategies for Reserves

There are four general funding strategies for association reserve accounts: baseline funding, threshold funding, full funding and statutory funding. Aside from statutory funding, the remaining three strategies are all about how much risk the association will be taking in funding their reserve account. Statutory funding is what associations need to have in reserves in order to comply with their state statutes. The other strategies would be at the association's discretion. Baseline funding looks at the future expenditures and their timing, and calculates future reserve contributions such that the reserve account balance will reach $0 as the lowest point over the life of the analysis, anywhere from 20 to 30 years out into the future. "This approach is the highest risk for the association to assume because it will get down to a $0 balance at some point," said Poehlmann. The threshold funding strategy is calculated like the baseline approach, with one very big difference — this plan never takes the reserve account balance down to $0. The reserve professional builds a cushion into the reserve account so that in the event that some capital expenditures are necessary sooner than projected in the association's reserve study, the association will have the available funds to cover those costs without having to conduct a special assessment or take out a bank loan. The last strategy, full funding, also known as the component method, is the least risky of the strategies, but there's a big tradeoff. "It's also the most costly," said Poehlmann. "What happens here is that each common element is looked at and funded individually. In other words, the association will begin fully funding for items that won't be replaced for up to 20 years." Poehlmann gave the example of the association's roofs. "Let's say they'll need to be replaced in 20 years at a cost of $200,000. In this example the association collects $10,000 per year and sets it aside. The money builds up over time and isn't used for 20 years. Now repeat this process with each of the association's common elements and before long, you're collecting a lot of money that won't be used for long periods of time," he said. This is the safest for the association, but is also significantly more costly than other strategies.

mon elements don't wear out overnight. Things change over time, like the inflation rate, interest earned on funds, etc. Every few years the study needs a fresh update to prevent the need for special assessments," he said.

Different Associations Need to Plan for Different Things

Poehlmann said that a good reserve study provider should ask questions about the objectives of the board and association in the reserve study. "We like to learn about what I call the 'culture' of the association. Some like to just maintain their properties while others take an active interest and want to maintain the association in ways that one might consider over-the-top, but others don't," he said. He gave an example of redecorating the clubhouse. "One association may want to do this every five years, because the members prefer to see it being kept as fresh as possible, while another association might redecorate only every 20 years. Neither is right or wrong, it's what I call the 'culture' of the association," he said.

Association board members have several roles in the reserve study process, and one of those roles is to communicate to the provider not only the list of common elements that should be included in the reserve study, but these types of desires for the association to maintain its individual personality.

Some Common Elements Frequently Overlooked by Associations

Asphalt seal coating is an example of one type of item that is frequently overlooked by associations. "Sometimes it's in the reserve account because of asphalt replacement, other times it's in the association's operating budget, and some of the time it's not anywhere to be found," said Poehlmann. When it's time to do it, the association will struggle to find the funds to do it, or take the money from the reserve account even though it wasn't part of the reserve budget. "Here's another one," he said. "This one's newer and particular to the northern part of the United States. In associations that have large numbers of ash trees on the property, we're looking at the invasion of the emerald ash borer that is attacking and killing significant numbers of ash trees. We'll incorporate the cost of ash tree removal and replacement with other species of trees if it's a large number and the board wants to reserve for it. Why not budget for it?"

The Sacred Funds — Keep Them Separate and Use as Planned

For the most part, the reserve funds should be kept in their own separate account. Statutes regarding this are different in each state, and the laws are frequently changing, so associations should ask their accounting and legal professionals about this. "It's really a legal question, and I'll defer to the attorneys," said Poehlmann. However, he pointed out an example of how Florida specifies the funds be kept. "In Florida, state law historically required that reserves for roofing be kept in a separate

> **What is cash flow analysis?**
>
> Poehlmann explained cash flow analysis as a method of calculating the appropriate level of reserve funding. It's also known as the pooling method. In short, using one of the cash flow methods, the reserve professional aggregates all of the future capital expenditures or project costs and "pools" them into one group. He then looks at those future capital expenditures as they come due and funds the reserves with consistent annual contributions into the reserve account with the objective that the reserve account will never fall into a deficit position or below a set minimum amount.

reserve account and could not be used for any other purpose than replacement of roofs," he said. More recently, this requirement has been relaxed. Other states allow using reserve money for other expenses, but specify the funds must be paid back to the reserve account within a strict time frame. Another factor in deciding how to keep and use reserves is the strategy the reserve study provider used to fund the reserve account. "One method, known as the cash flow method or pooling method, pools all of the future replacement costs into a pool. That pool of funds is used to conduct the replacements in the order that they come due," said Poehlmann.

Is There Ever Anything Leftover — What if We Overfund?

Poehlmann said there really is no such thing as leftover reserves. A reserve account is a dynamic thing. It's constantly changing, money goes into it (reserve contributions) and money is drawn from it (paying for capital projects) on a regular basis. "And remember, the association never completely wears out, so the purpose of and need for the reserve account never comes to an end," he explained.

At some point, if a reserve account has been overfunded over a period of time, the board could then reduce the regular common fees assessed to the owners. However, associations should beware of and avoid overfunding the account. "The negative aspect of overfunding is that the current owners are paying more than their fair share into the reserve account. This means that, as the current owners are paying too much, the future boards will reduce the amount of reserve assessments and the future owners will pay less into the reserve account because today's owners are paying for part of the future necessary contribution," said Poehlmann. So, in essence, when you overfund, the current owners are paying toward a future fee reduction that, if they move, they will never be able to enjoy. And additionally, owners who purchase later in this timeline will not be contributing the same level of funding toward the reserve account as current owners.

"Regular reserve study updates will help keep the association on track," said Poehlmann. These should be conducted every three years to avoid overfunding, or possibly worse, underfunding. Reserve study updates account for changes in the inflation rate of materials and labor, interest rate changes on the reserve funds and accelerating or delaying capital projects as compared to the original reserve plan estimates. "All of these events contribute to the calculation of an appropriate level of reserve funding," he said.

How Much Should a Reserve Study Cost?

According to Poehlmann, the prices vary on reserve studies, and there is even software that associations can purchase to do simplified, but not very reliable, reserve studies. However, cost should not be the main factor in choosing a reserve study provider. He also does not recommend relying on do-it-yourself software for this important service. Poehlmann said to look at the choice of which provider to use from a board member's perspective. "What do I, as a board member, want out of that study? I want the kind of reserve study that will help me fulfill my fiduciary responsibility, protect the investment of the association members in their homes, provide our board with advice and recommendations that would save the homeowners money over the long run and educate us so that we can be more effective board members while maintaining a community where the members look forward to coming home every night," he said. For the most part, board members are neighbors in the communities they serve, and they should treat the decision about how to pursue maintaining proper reserves in terms of how it would affect their neighbors and themselves.

What is typically included in the cost of a reserve study? CAI and the APRA have strict guidelines as to the minimum components of what should be included the reserve study. "National standards were developed in the mid 1990s by a small committee of national reserve study providers, of which I was fortunate enough to be one," said Poehlmann. One can expect, at a minimum, a component inventory of each common element, a physical inspection and measurement of each common element, a determination of the normal useful life of each, the remaining life (how long before replacement is necessary), a status of the reserve fund at the time of the reserve study, and a funding plan that determines the amount of annual reserve contributions necessary to offset the anticipated expenditures for replacement over at least the next 20 years. "That's the minimum," he said.

How Have Reserve Studies Changed Over Time?

Poehlmann said that reserve studies have changed in many ways over the past few decades. "My partner, Ted Salgado, and I started conducting reserve studies in the 1980s, which was only about 15 to 20 years from the birth of the community association industry," he said. "We've seen a lot of changes over the years. In the early days, we found that most people who were doing reserve studies were property managers or board members because there wasn't a reserve study industry yet. Property components were just beginning to wear out and associations clearly weren't prepared for that. They'd take projections from contractors and guesstimate the future replacement costs in very unscientific ways. We'd see accountants trying to get their arms around the question of how to fund for replacements. People were using different terminology in different parts of the country. Some were providing engineering inspection reports that were invasive in nature, providing more information than a board would ever need to plan for the future. Others were providing common element replacement forecasts without any kind of funding plan, which didn't really help when it came time to budget. They still called these reserve studies, even though half of what we expect from reserve studies today wasn't even included."

Poehlmann said in the mid-1990s, CAI invited Salgado and him, along with a handful of other reserve study providers, to meet and develop national reserve study standards and consistent terminology so boards and managers would have a basis from which to compare providers and have reasonable expectations of what they were buying. "Along with that came the Reserve Specialist designation program that required providers to provide their reserve studies in accordance with these standards. The purpose of the national standards was to provide boards with a standard reserve study that served as a budgeting tool," he said.

Going forward, Poehlmann sees the industry expanding. "More states will enact legislation to ensure that associations are protecting their members' investments in their homes. Other factors, such as green technologies and new materials will also have an impact on reserve studies. Additionally, new technologies and methods are continually being developed to make the reserve studies even more accurate and informative. We think the reserve study industry is about to take the next exciting step in its evolution," said Poehlmann.

9

Association Loans

Under what conditions may an association need to apply for a bank loan? Who is responsible for paying the loan? Can board members or homeowners be held responsible in the case of default? What are the benefits, if any, of taking out a loan as opposed to using reserves to fund projects? What are the terms generally for association loans?

There are infinite questions involving association borrowing, but your first one may be "When, on earth, would an association need to apply for a bank loan?" Management and the board are supposed to be ensuring there are adequate reserves, right? If my HOA is applying for a loan, does that mean we're in dire trouble and the association is mismanaged? The answer to that question could be yes or no, depending on a few different factors. However, associations do not only seek loans because they're mismanaged or low on reserves. Fortunately, Thomas Engblom, CMCA, AMS, PCAM, VP/Regional Account Executive at Mutual of Omaha Bank, availed himself to answer these questions for our readers.

The best place to start talking about association loans is to describe what an association may need a loan for? According to Engblom, the reason for and types of loans are geographically driven and depend on what type of physical property the association is comprised of. The loan can be for roof replacements, paving, siding, carpeting for the halls of a building with interior residence entrances, decorating of a clubhouse or lobby, adding a pool, adding a clubhouse — the list goes on. An association could obtain a loan for any number of capital repairs or improvements to buildings and common areas.

Financing litigation against the developer and manufacturers of building materials to remedy construction defects is another reason an association may need to obtain a loan. An HOA loan can be the best way to fund a construction defect litigation suit, as the loan can help the association through the process by funding both legal fees and building costs until the suit is settled — which can take several years.

Additionally, an association's bylaws or declaration may have imposed requirements that prevented the association from securing and maintaining adequate reserves for their actual needs. Or these documents may impose a minimum amount that needs to be maintained in reserves. Therefore, those funds cannot be used at the time the funds are needed.

So who is responsible for paying this loan, and are unit owners on the line for the money if the association doesn't pay on time? Can the bank place liens on the individual units for the loan? Unit-owners are only in-

☞ Loans Can Offer Cost Savings in the Long Run

Rather than taking out a loan, what if an association decided to replace the roofs in their community over a five-year period, which could be paid from their current assessments? Is there a disadvantage to doing this as opposed to financing the project and doing it all at once? Engblom said that it is generally more cost-effective to replace all the roofs at the same time, as the cost per unit will be lower when purchasing in bulk. Additionally, there is the added benefit of having everything done at once, and having all the units in the community with roofs of the same age. This makes it less likely that additional problems with the roofs will surface during the project if it were to span a five-year period. It also helps plan for future replacements more easily.

directly responsible for the loan. Unlike a mortgage or home equity loan, the association loan is not secured by any physical elements of the community, including the individual units and common elements. Instead, an

> ### How Much to Borrow?
>
> Let's say an association is applying for a loan to redecorate the hallways of its high-rise building. They have a proposal from the company they plan to use to do the project, but how do they determine the amount to borrow? What if there are unexpected costs that come up during the project? Engblom recommended applying for a loan that is 20% greater than the amount needed for a particular project. He explained that the way association loans are structured, there is a draw period, during which the work is usually done. Therefore, the association doesn't need to draw — that is borrow — the extra funds if they are not needed. Associations should do this because it is more difficult to go back to the bank after a loan is closed to request additional funds. Doing that would be viewed as a loan modification, which should be avoided by the association. That is why it is very important to have accurate figures, and then leave some room for the unexpected when procuring your loan.

association loan is secured by the future assessments to be collected by the association. Additionally, there are no personal guarantors on the association loan, so board members are also not personally responsible for paying the loan.

What are the terms commonly assigned to association loans? Engblom said that the amount of an association loan can be anywhere from $50,000 to $50 million, and several factors will determine the length of the time for which the loan should be cast. This depends on the life expectancy of what is being financed. However, it also depends on the board, and the individual association, and includes factors such as how the association plans to fund those payments. For example, the board can actually special assess the unit-owners in order to repay the loan. In this case, the board can give unit-owners a choice of paying this special assessment as one large amount upfront, or they can pay over a specified period of time with an additional amount to be paid for interest. The board can raise their monthly or annual assessments to pay the loan.

Either way, terms for an association loan are typically 5, 7, 10 or 15 years. Again, these terms would depend on the project to be financed. According to Engblom, most association loans are actually paid before their term period expires. For example, he said, a 5-year loan is typically paid in 3 years, a 10-year loan is paid in 7. And defaults are very rare in association loans. Engblom noted that association loans are a fairly new phenomenon — only being around for about 15 years. And he said that they are among the safest types of loans for banks to issue to customers.

The last component of the loan would be determining the interest rate. This is typically determined by the United States Treasury rate.

> **Do banks require any documentation from the residents in the approval process of the association loan?**
>
> Engblom said no, the residents and board members are not asked to provide personal information, such as personal tax returns, when the association is applying for a loan. Nor are the credit ratings of residents viewed. However, residents do indirectly affect the association's ability to obtain a loan if they develop a history of paying their assessments late or allowing their units to go into foreclosure.

So what is required by the bank from the association when applying for a loan? According to Engblom, banks typically look at a number of items which help them determine if they can provide the loan to the association. One important factor is the association fee delinquency rate. The bank will examine this over a period, typically, of 4 months, and usually require there to be fewer than 10% delinquencies in the community. This would include units with accounts over 60 days past due. Additionally, it is common for the loan documents to have language that states that, during the repayment of the loan, the association maintain this desired, low fee delinquency rate. Since these common fees are the only collateral for an association loan, the security of these is very important to the lender.

Another important factor is the size of the association. This will affect its ability to obtain a loan. In referring to association size, typically banks will say "the bigger the better," when an association is applying for a loan. Look at it this way, the more units in an association, the more the payments will be spread out over a larger number of owners who indirectly affect the repayment of the loan. According to Engblom, communities with less than 25 units will face some challenges in applying for funding from a bank.

The bank also looks at the number of investor-owned units in the community. According to Engblom, if a community has greater than 40% of its units owned by investors who rent those units, that community will have greater challenges with an association loan. Also, if one person owns a large portion of the units or has a large proportion of the voting control of the community, the association will not be approved for a loan.

Lastly, does having a loan on the books of the association affect the owners' property values or cause the association to be viewed in a negative manner? This question can be viewed in a number of ways and depends on many factors. However, if the loan prevents the property and/or its common elements from deteriorating, such as if the loan prevents putting off necessary projects, which could lead to structural problems or worse, the loan can help maintain or even bolster property values. Additionally, in cases where a loan prevents special assessments or fee increases, residents maintain their personal cash to preserve quality of life, and even have more available funds to put into their own individual units. Having well-maintained and updated units helps bolster property values as well.

10

Association Insurance — Ensuring You're Protected

Insurance is a complex subject in any context, and in the realm of community associations — condominiums and homeowners associations (HOAs) — there are many bases to cover when it comes to ensuring the association, its board, manager and residents are all appropriately protected. We spoke with Scott Breslin from McCredie Insurance Agency, Inc., in Flint, Michigan, and Robert Travis, CIRMS, CPIA from the Newtown, Pennsylvania, office of Community Association Underwriters of America, Inc. (CAU), a national insurance company which specializes exclusively in insuring community associations and other common interest properties.

So how does a community determine how much and what types of insurance are needed? While an association's governing documents offer meticulous details about the governance of a community, they don't typically, and shouldn't according to Travis, specify exact amounts of insurance needed. However, they usually lay the groundwork for building the proper mix of coverage. "They're going to have an impact in setting minimal standards of insurance for every line of insurance the association needs to have," he said. The types of insurance needed by associations are Property, Directors & Officers (D&O) Liability, Fidelity (otherwise known as Employee Dishonesty), Commercial General Liability, Workers' Compensation and Commercial Umbrella. "The governing documents can have a lot to say, and have a strong demand about what the minimal level of insurance will be," he said.

The association also needs to be comfortable that they're fulfilling all the insurance requirements of federal and state statutes, and any contractual or lenders' requirements. Above that, boards need to fulfill their business judgment — that is, ensure they're fulfilling their fiduciary duty and exercising due care in their decisions — to make sure they have adequate coverage. But Travis noted there is no definitive answer as to how much is too much when discussing insurance. "No one can know what the future could bring in terms of losses," he said.

Property Insurance

Homeowners should note that there is different insurance needed depending on whether their community is a condominium association or an HOA.

In covering the properties in condominium associations, there is a master insurance policy for the association, then individual unit owners have their own insurance — commonly called HO6 policies — which cover their individual unit's contents as well as any upgrades made to the unit by the owner or previous owner. These policies also cover things such as additional living expenses, special assessments caused by a loss to the association, as well as giving General Liability coverage to the owner.

What should an association know about how its master policy interacts with the coverage residents have on their individual units? The first thing people need to understand is that, when it comes to insuring the unit in a condominium, the association's insurance is always primary. When a loss occurs, the unit owner's insurer is always going to look and see how the master policy dispenses of the claim, and then their HO6 policy — the unit owner's policy — will step in and cover what it can pick up after the association's master policy applies to the claim first.

Here is an example of how this works. Let's say there is a storm and a medium-sized tree falls on the roof of a two-story condominium building. While no major damage is done to the structure, the roof is torn causing water to leak into the kitchen of the unit below. The unit's ceiling collects water and the sheetrock eventually breaches, causing a hole in the unit's ceiling and water damage to the custom wood cabinetry the owner had installed after the original purchase of the unit from the developer. The condominium's master policy pays to repair the roof and the ceiling inside the condo unit. Then the unit owner's HO-6 policy picks up the cost to replace the custom cabinetry that was not part of the original unit sold by the developer.

Another example of how the HO-6 policy kicks in is when there is minor damage that is under the amount of the deductible of the association's master policy. Then the HO-6 policy picks up the repair cost, making the unit owner whole again subject to the HO-6 deductible.

Travis emphasized that having an overlap of coverage in these cases is better than having a gap in coverage. "Don't think of this adding up to 100% of the value. Having a little bit of overlapping coverage is a far better scenario than putting yourself in a position where you may have a gap," he said.

With HOAs, on the other hand, sometimes the association is covering the unit and sometimes it's not. That would depend on the association's governing documents. In townhome communities, even where there are common roofs, it is not always the case that the association's master policy will cover the townhome building. Homeowners should have their insurance professionals make sure they have reviewed the governing documents and offer the proper coverage for their particular situation.

When insuring a property, it is best to be covered for the Replacement Cost Valuation (RCV) of what is insured. What is meant by Replacement Cost Valuation as opposed to an item's Actual Cash Value (ACV)? When evaluating a loss, Actual Cash Value takes depreciation into consideration. Travis gave an example of someone who has a seventeen-year-old Plymouth Neon. Let's say this person has Comprehensive and Collision Coverage on this car and has a total loss of the car in an accident. The insurance company will pay an amount to purchase another seventeen-year-old Plymouth Neon. That is Actual Cash Value. Inversely, Replacement Cost Valuation does not take depreciation into consideration. So a policy that is written to cover Replacement Cost Valuation will pay an amount for this person to buy a brand-new Neon. "So Actual Cash Value is a valuation where it is replacement cost, minus depreciation," he said. "It does not give you enough money to rebuild a building, it gives you the depreciated value of that building."

Associations need to make sure they regularly check their insurer's estimate of the replacement value for their property to ensure they have enough coverage. How often should this be done? "In my opinion," said Travis, "annually." He recommended the association get a Replacement Cost Valuation from an actual replacement cost construction valuation company, and enter into a contract for the company to come back on a regular basis, such as every three years. Then during the in-between years, Travis said that you should get an automatic increase based on construction cost increases at the time in that geographic area. He said that the valuation company can provide you with this as well.

Associations should also be knowledgeable of their property's replacement value in connection with its property insurance policy's co-insurance clause. Otherwise they could be subject to a co-insurance penalty should a loss occur. The co-insurance clause basically puts a condition upon the insured that they are properly insuring the premises to its true replacement value. The actual percentage of insurance required varies from company to company. "The co-insurance clause basically will state that if an insured does not properly insure the building or buildings to the proper percentage of the true replacement value, that they will then be penalized on any and all claims on the property," he said.

For example, let's say someone has a building worth $100,000 from a replacement cost standpoint, and their insurance policy has an eighty-percent co-insurance clause — it's saying that this person or association should at least be insuring the building for $80,000 on a replacement cost basis. If they choose to insure it for an RCV of $70,000, the insurance company is then going to do an evaluation at the time of the loss and discover that the building is worth $100,000 and is only insured for $70,000. Therefore, the building is only insured for 7/8ths of what the co-insurance clause specifies. Consequently, the insurer can rightly say they're only going to pay 7/8ths of any loss.

Travis explained if the person or association in the above example had a total loss, they would only be paid 7/8ths of the policy limit of $70,000. "That's how the co-insurance penalty works," he said.

"Ordinance or Law coverage is also a very important aspect of Property coverage that cannot be overlooked," Scott Breslin said. He further explained that Ordinance or Law coverage includes three insurance agreements: coverage A, coverage B, and coverage C. Coverage A replaces the portion of the building that is not damaged in a coverage loss. "Municipalities have laws that state that, if a building is destroyed by more than fifty percent, the undamaged portion must be torn down and the entire building rebuilt," Breslin said. Coverage B refers to demolition cost, which pays for the cost to demolish the undamaged portion of the building. Coverage C refers to the increased cost of construction. Coverage C comes into play if a municipality requires that building codes be updated.

Board Members & Managers — Make Sure You're Covered: D&O Liability Insurance

Associations need to have special insurance to cover themselves and their board members in case they're sued in relation to their actions in running the community. Board members can be sued for any wrongful acts or breach of their fiduciary duties to the association. A breach of fiduciary duty is going to be whenever a board member or any other person of authority in a community association does not properly exercise the proper controls or procedures in handling and utilizing the community association funds. "If I'm a board member and I am putting the association into contracts that they don't really need to be in, I'm forcing money to be spent that doesn't need to be spent, or I'm mishandling funds, that is a breach of my fiduciary duty. I have a fiduciary duty to protect the association's funds," said Travis.

A breach of fiduciary duty can also include when board members, or the manager, do not properly protect the assets of the association, including the resale value of the lots, units and homes in the association. "When you have a breach of fiduciary duty you're not fulfilling the fiduciary duty that you have to protect the money of the community association and its membership," he said.

This is where Directors & Officers (D&O) liability insurance comes in. A D&O liability policy is designed to protect the association from various wrongful acts of its board members and association leadership. These wrong-

Waiver of Subrogation — Protecting Boards from Potential Liability

What is a waiver of subrogation? Most states have this written into their statutes or their condominium acts. In the world of community associations, the waiver of subrogation basically means that the association waives its right to subrogate: that is specifically to go after a unit owner when the unit owner causes a loss or claim for the community association. Travis gave the following example: "I live in an eight-unit condominium and I'm in my unit and I fall asleep while smoking a cigarette and that cigarette then falls and sets my mattress on fire. I get out alive and I get everyone else out alive, but all eight units burn down to the ground. What the waiver of subrogation is going to stipulate is that the community association is not going to be able to come after me to rebuild all eight of those units." This also means that the association's insurer cannot go after the person in this example. The association and its property insurance need to pay this on their own, and they cannot subrogate against the unit owner.

Travis explained that the reason why the waiver of subrogation was written into the early condominium statues was to take certain decisions out of the board's hands. Take an example of two unit owners having the same type of loss. Each of their water heaters burst and the result is $10,000 worth of damage to each of their buildings. Let's say one of the unit owners is well-liked by the board. He volunteers on committees, he is a good neighbor and always participates positively in association meetings. The other unit owner, however, is the bane of the board's existence. He causes disturbances at meetings and frequently calls the board president to harass him. In this example you can see where this law protects the board from inadvertently making an arbitrary decision to sue one of the owners and possibly not the other due to their personal feelings about either individual. Because of the waiver of subrogation, one does not need to decide if an owner should be sued in these cases, as the association's master policy pays the claim. Travis explained that, while insurance companies have lost large amounts of money due to paying claims in cases where waiver of subrogation applies, it would have been much worse if they didn't have the law because, he said, they would be paying even more in D&O liability claims.

ful acts can come in two categories. One is monetary losses — where someone sues an association for a wrongful act which has cost the claimant a dollar amount. Or, someone can sue a board of directors for a non-monetary claim. This is where they're suing not for a dollar amount, but for injunctive relief. "It's easy to say that most D&O claims are of the non-monetary variety," said Travis. In cases seeking injunctive relief, it is when someone sues the board because they feel the board is enforcing a rule that is working unfairly against them. They want to go to court and have the court tell the board they must stop enforcing the rule in question. The opposite could also be the case. An individual can take the board to court saying that they're not properly enforcing a rule. "They're trying to get the court to make the board actually enforce the rule," he said. So in these cases, the board is not being sued for a monetary amount, but in order to make them take some action, or to stop them from taking an action they are taking. In the non-monetary suits, the costs that need to be covered are all for legal defense.

> **Don't Be Afraid to Join the Board — The Indemnification Clause**
>
> The indemnification clause is typically found in the association's bylaws, and it states that if a board member is sued through their actions functioning as such, the community association shall indemnify the board member and reimburse them for any financial loss. Travis said that the purpose of the indemnification clause is basically to address the fears many people have about stepping up to serve on the board of their association. Many individuals are afraid to volunteer as board members for fear of the potential liability. "The indemnification clause is going to try and encourage people to take association leadership positions by telling them 'hey, if you make a decision out here and you get personally named in a lawsuit, have expenses with the lawsuit and you lose the lawsuit, the association will indemnify you,'" he said.
>
> When the association buys D&O liability insurance, it should be a policy that will be able to back up that promise. Travis warned, if the proper policy isn't written, then the association would need to write a check out of its own pocket to back up this indemnification promise.

Obviously, lawsuits can arise even when board members are fulfilling their fiduciary duties and following the rules of their associations to the letter. Travis explained that boards are faced with many difficult decisions, of which, whatever choice is made could have some undesired effect for some residents. "Every day goes by where a situation is posed to a community association insurance professional, and we look at it and we know that the board was between a rock and a hard place. That either decision you could back up as being a prudent decision, but either way you made a decision you're setting yourself up for detractors and a possible lawsuit from those who think it's the wrong decision," said Travis. So even if every step of the way you're trying to do the best you can do, many decisions that need to be made have no ideal choice that will satisfy everyone in the community. Even if there are two desirable choices in a decision, someone could say you chose the wrong one. "Even if you have the very best risk-management program on earth, you still do not eliminate all potential exposure to loss," said Travis.

Are there things the D&O policy won't cover? Travis said yes. One example is if someone is making a decision as a board member that helps them put money in their own pocket — such as if they sway jobs to a company the board member has a financial interest in, thereby profiting himself. Certain events are going to be excluded from D&O coverage. "If it's criminal, if it is lining your own pockets, or something similar to these acts, there are just certain things that are not covered and certain types of wrongful acts that are not going to be covered," he said.

Another item that possibly may not be covered by a D&O policy is when the board is accused of a wrongful act that is considered to be discriminatory toward someone in a protected class. According to Travis, there are some D&O policies that provide no protection for discrimination whatsoever. Alternatively, some D&O policies provide defense costs only, and then there are some that will not only provide defense costs but will also pay judgments made against the association for a discrimination claim. Travis said that there are different types of coverage available to boards and they should be sure they choose the D&O policy that protects their exposures to loss.

A somewhat gray area of coverage is the mismanagement or improper investment of funds. In terms of mismanagement or improper investment of the association's funds, Travis noted this is a very broad topic. "For the most part, most D&O policies are not going to provide any coverage for mismanagement or improper investment of funds," he said, "but some do." He explained further that if you're getting into areas where the FDIC is not providing insurance for your monies while they're sitting in an investment fund, the D&O policy might not provide coverage either.

One thing board members should be aware of is that D&O is not there for Bodily Injury or Property Damage losses. That's what General Liability insurance is for. "If I'm going to sue a board because I got hurt, or I'm going to sue them because my property or my car was damaged, and I blame the board for my injury or my damage, that is not a D&O lawsuit, that is going to be a General Liability lawsuit," he said. D&O does not get into the Bodily Injury, Property Damage arena.

How do board members determine how much D&O insurance they require? First, most states have something about this in their statutes. After referring to state guidelines, the next place to look is their own governing documents — the declaration, CC&Rs, articles of incorporation and the bylaws. "Someplace within the declaration, the articles of incorporation or the bylaws there may be some minimal standards set out as to what limits the board should have as far as directors and officers liability," said Travis. He added that there also may be lenders, such as Fannie Mae, Freddie Mac, or the FHA and HUD that require certain limits in order to comply with those lending institutions. There could be another type of contract also demanding a certain amount of coverage, such as that with a local municipality or neighboring property whereby there may be a cooperative venture. "After that," he said, "then it becomes a business judgment." So an association may evaluate their assets and decide to have additional insurance based on that value, rather than going with the minimum required by other entities.

Board members should make sure they're named as an additional insured on the association's D&O liability policy. "The community association is going to be what's called the first named insured. The first named insured is the party that's on the policy's declaration page," he said. All the other insureds, such as the board members, committee members and managers, are named in the body of the policy. "Those are the folks who are additional insureds," he said. This ensures that if there is a lawsuit, and these board members are named along with the association, that they will be covered by the policy.

Board members should verify that they are, in fact, insured under the association's D&O policy by asking to see a copy of the policy. "If I'm a board member and I have someone whose opinion I value, such as my insurance agent or attorney, I'm getting a copy of the association's D&O policy and asking what they think about it. Quite frankly, I'm also reading it myself," he said. Other than doing that, a board member would be relying on certificates of insurance and proposals, and Travis said that not even the most comprehensive proposal explains every exclusion or definition on a policy. For example, every D&O policy covers for wrongful acts, however, every policy also has its own definition of what a wrongful act is. "That's the definition that the entire policy is hitched up to," he said, "so I would want to see that definition of wrongful acts."

Other Protection for Board Members & Managers

Aside from the D&O policy, the board members should expect to have protection for their General Liability coverage. This would be for scenarios where they might get individually sued for a Bodily Injury or Property Damage to a third party that may find them individually responsible. "As an example, if I'm the head of the social committee and somebody gets hurt at one of the social events, they may sue the community association, but then sue me. As an individual I need to make sure that I have that kind of protection from my community association as a volunteer," he said. Board members should expect to have coverage if they're individually sued in this manner.

Property managers should follow a similar procedure in ensuring they're insured in this manner. Travis recommended the manager make sure they are a named insured on all the General Liability and D&O liability policies that are written for all the community associations that they manage. Managers should also make sure that their management company, the site manager themselves and other management company employees are insureds on the policy as well.

Fidelity Insurance

This brings us to protecting associations, boards and managers in cases of theft of association funds. Fidelity insurance, which covers things such as employee theft, should be in place for this purpose. Travis explained that, for the most part, this is purchased to protect the association from something an employee could potentially steal. Travis explained that a contractor would buy this type of coverage because they're worried about an employee stealing their tools and equipment. A retailer could be worried about employees stealing their goods. Community associations, however, are primarily concerned with people stealing the association's funds. "The average community association really doesn't have what you and I would define as an employee. So in a community association environment we need to expand the definition of an employee so that it not only includes the kind of employee the IRS defines as an employee, but it also includes board members, committee members and volunteers operating within the scope of the direction of the association," he said. He added that if the association is professionally managed, they need to make sure the site manager, the management company and all its employees are included in the definition of employee on the Fidelity policy as well. The policy is intended to protect for potential internal theft of community association monies.

General Liability Insurance

As you can see the mix of policies procured by an association work together in a variety of ways. We've touched a bit on the General Liability insurance policy. So, what is General Liability insurance?

General Liability, like D&O, responds to what are called third party claims. These are when a third party, someone other than the community association or the insurer, makes a claim or lawsuit against a community association claiming that the third party has somehow been injured or suffered damage because of the community association's actions or lack thereof. There are basically four parts to General Liability.

The first of these four is Bodily Injury. Bodily Injury is when someone has a physical injury to their person and claims the association is at fault.

The next item covered under General Liability is Property Damage. This is when someone has property that has been damaged, and they either have direct physical damage, or indirect damage, meaning loss of use

> **Beware of Potential Liquor Liability**
>
> Community associations can get themselves into trouble if they decide to charge for liquor at such an event. In that case, an association may need to obtain a liquor license and then can't be covered by the Host Liquor Liability coverage. In that case, an association would need Dram Shop Liquor Liability — that is, true Liquor Liability insurance.

of a property, and that direct or indirect damage or loss is claimed to be the community association's fault.

Then there is Personal Injury. Not to be confused with Bodily Injury, this is when the community association is sued for something the association has said or done, which has hurt someone's reputation or self-worth. Personal injury in this context is not when someone is physically injured.

Advertising Injury, said Travis, is the same as Personal Injury, except it's in the written or published form. "So when we say things about people in board minutes or on the association's website, we are talking about two classic examples of Advertising Injury exposure," he said.

Under the General Liability policy, associations should include Host Liquor Liability insurance. This is for the Liquor Liability exposure an association has when hosting a party or event, since they are not in the business of selling alcohol. This is for those situations where a liquor license is not needed, because liquor won't be sold, but it is being served at no charge or given away. These situations include wine and cheese parties, picnic type parties, cocktail parties — or any event where liquor will be provided in this manner. This type of insurance needs to be added to the General Liability policy.

Workers' Compensation Insurance

Not every association has employees, however, every association should have workers' compensation insurance coverage. Travis said that every community association should have Workers' Compensation coverage, whether or not it has employees, to cover contractors who are sole proprietors or partnerships. Travis explained that in most states, sole proprietors and partners in partnerships are unable to purchase Workers' Compensation insurance to cover themselves. They are required to purchase it to cover their employees, and they will produce an insurance certificate to show the association they have the coverage for those employees. However the sole proprietor or partner in most states cannot cover himself under that policy. The reason being is that sole proprietors or partners are not considered employees of themselves. So if the sole proprietor or partner himself were to be injured on the job site, his Workers' Compensation coverage would not cover him or her. What often will happen in the Workers' Compensation courts is that since the sole proprietor or partner isn't covered under his own policy, they will look at whom he was working for on the day he was injured. If they determine that the sole proprietor or partner was working for the community association that day as an employee, the association now owes Workers' Compensation benefits for that sole proprietor or partner.

Another reason to have Workers' Compensation coverage is to provide coverage in case one of their contractors provides a false certificate of insurance. If one of these contractor employees is injured on the job and the contractor has no Workers' Compensation Insurance, the Workers' Compensation courts would likely deem the association responsible for the Workers' Compensation claim. Again, they would look at whom the individual was working for the day he was injured much like the scenario described in the previous paragraph.

Travis said that yet another reason why it is needed is to provide coverage for casual labor. The association could casually pay a teen to clean up a small area around the association's pond on a Saturday, for example, and pay him or her $50 out of petty cash. The association's Workers' Compensation coverage would apply here if that teen were injured while performing this casual labor. "The Workers' Compensation courts are going to look at this as an employee/employer relationship," he said.

So for these reasons, even if a community association has no payroll, they should have Workers' Compensation coverage.

Specific Coverage For Associations with Employees

As for associations that do have employees, they should carry a type of coverage to protect board members and association assets against employee claims.

There are three types of employee coverage and claims that would come up here.

There is Employment Practices Liability, which is when the association or the board can get sued for how they practice being an employer. This includes hiring and firing, as well as how employees are treated on the job, raises, promotions and more. "Generally we get that coverage from our D&O liability policy," said Travis. He explained that the D&O policy's Part B is usually Employment Practices Liability when the D&O policy does provide this coverage.

Next is Workers' Compensation coverage, discussed previously, which covers the association should an employee get hurt during a work-related incident. These benefits are required and determined by the state.

Then there is a second part of the Workers' Compensation policy, called Employer's Liability, which is for when an injured employee waives their rights to be taken care of by the Workers' Compensation system, and they want to sue their employer for some additional funds. "That would be Part B of the Workers' Compensation policy," said Travis. He further explained that when an employee sues in this manner, waiving Workers' Compensation coverage, not only does the employee have to prove that they were injured on the job, but that their injury was the result of their employer's negligence.

The Commercial Umbrella — Covering the Coverage

As I'm sure you all know, an Commercial Umbrella policy is not a special policy to cover the umbrellas around your community's swimming pool. This is an important liability policy that covers above and beyond other liability policies. "If you had a General Liability policy that had $1 million per occurrence and $2 million in the aggregate, and you had a $10 million Commercial Umbrella and you were to suffer a $5 million loss, then the General Liability policy is going to basically take the first $1 million. Then the Commercial Umbrella policy is going to cover the next $4 million above that," Travis explained.

The Commercial Umbrella policy sits on top of your General Liability policy. It will also go over your D&O policy and any other liability coverage the association purchases. The Commercial Umbrella would help in case a claim goes over the limits of any of these policies. "It basically provides excess coverage to the limits that are shown in all of the underlying liability policies that are listed on the Commercial Umbrella policy's declaration page," he said.

When Can Associations Self-Insure?

Self-insurance is any scenario where an entity or community association could buy insurance, but decides not to. In these cases, the entity or community retains the risk, and if anything comes up, they would be the ones to pay for the loss and/or legal defense. Travis explained that to be self-insured is a two-step process. First, there needs to be insurance that can be purchased for that exposure. Then if there's insurance that can be purchased for that exposure, the association makes the choice not to buy that insurance. They choose instead to take financial responsibility if something happens.

"If it was an uninsurable event," he said, "then you're not self-insuring and it's just a business expense." Events that are not insurable would include things like repairing the roads after a bad winter. Since there is no insurance that covers this, an association cannot be self-insured for it, and must absorb the cost as a business expense. "Self-insurance is when you could have bought insurance, and made the decision not to buy insurance," he said. That is the act of self-insurance.

Do You Valet?

One special type of coverage that may be needed by some associations would be Garage Keepers insurance. Garage Keepers insurance covers when an association has someone else's automobile in their care, custody and control. This could be if an association has unit-owners' automobiles kept in an area under the care, custody and control of the association. For example, lots of community associations, especially in urban areas, have valet parking only. So residents and guests pull up to the building, give the valet their keys and they park the car in the garage for you. "That is the ultimate example of your car being in the care, custody and control of the community association, not you. That is a classic example of when you need what they call Garage Keepers insurance," said Travis. This type of policy enables associations to insure vehicles they don't own for when they are in their custody.

Checking the Insurance Carrier's Rating

Associations can check an insurance company's ratings in order to gauge the strength of the company and their ability to pay claims. Checking the AM Best Rating of the company is the best way to do this. It is an independent party's evaluation of what position they are in financially to pay a claim. Travis said you can refer to other sources for the ratings as well, such as Moody's or Standard & Poors. "There are several companies that evaluate an insurance company's ability to pay future claims," said Travis.

11

Association Accounting and Budgets

When it comes to the association's finances, how can boards be assured they're handling things properly? Where should the board begin when creating budgets? What are the reporting requirements and rules for handling association funds? What are the proper accounting methods? How can an association be assured they don't become the victims of theft or fraud when it comes to their funds? We spoke with Linda Strussione, CPA of Owens and Strussione PC in Shelby Township, Michigan to answer these questions and enlighten readers on other important accounting topics.

Accounting Methods

There are two different accounting methods, cash and accrual. Which is the best one for associations? According to Strussione, accrual works best for associations. She explained the reason for this is that it follows the American Institute of Certified Public Accountant's (AICPA's) requirement that at least the annual report at the end of the year be on an accrual basis. So accrual basis accounting follows the AICPA ruling on non-profit associations. "That's how it has to be reported," she said. Strussione explained that cash basis accounting only recognizes income and expenses if they actually happen. But accrual basis accounting is the technically correct method because it recognizes expenses in the fiscal year they occur, whether they're paid or not. Accrual basis accounting also recognizes income in the year it was supposed to be collected, whether it's collected or not. This method gives the association a true picture of what the income and expenses were for a particular fiscal year.

Strussione said there is, in fact, a professional requirement for how the accounting is done. In Michigan, if an accountant is doing audits or reviews, they are required to follow the AICPA Peer Review guidelines. This mandates that reports be done on an accrual basis.

Organizing Budgets

When creating the association's budget, of course it makes sense to categorize expenses. What is the best way to categorize these, and how detailed should the categories be?

Strussione explained that there are certain categories that are commonly used, and within those are sub-categories, which break the main category into greater detail. The first category associations typically list is the "Administrative" section. Within that section there will be sub-groupings such as office, legal, professional, accounting, paper, postage, etc. The second category that would appear on a typical association budget is "Operating Expenses" — which includes things such as utilities and rubbish removal. The third category seen on a typical budget is "Repairs & Maintenance." This category can be as detailed as is needed, and include anything having to do with interior or exterior maintenance and repairs. "Sometimes the more detailed the better," said Strussione. If an association has a clubhouse, they can have a fourth category of expenses for that. "We recommend they keep that separate so they know exactly how much the clubhouse is costing," she said. After this, Strussione recommends having a category for "Reserve Expenses." This is where the association predicts what their reserve withdrawal expenses will be used for during that year. The last category would be "Insurance & Taxes." These are the main categories Strussione recommends for boards creating budgets. Those main categories can be expanded further using sub-categories. Strussione again stressed that "the more detailed, the better."

The advantage of having detailed sub-categories is that they allow an association to see exactly what expenses they are estimating every year. "For example, in the Repairs and Maintenance category, you could have something like cement, or window replacement. You're going to have large ticket items that go through the operating expenses, but they don't necessarily occur every year," she said. The Repairs and Maintenance category is sometimes 80% of the total budget. The more detailed the budget is, the more you will see what you are paying for. "You're always going to have some fixed expenses, but you're going to have variable costs that come up," said Strussione.

How often should the budget be analyzed and by whom? The budget is the responsibility of the board of directors. There is usually a lot of support from the association's manager or management company, but the board is ultimately responsible. Strussione recommended reviewing the budget 3-6 months prior to the end of the association's fiscal year, but she also said that you should look at it throughout the year. "If they're gathering data and trying to figure out what they need to do for the next calendar or fiscal year, if they're expecting their expenses to go up or down, or determine what major expenditures may be incurred in the next fiscal year, I recommend they look at their budget at least three times a year," she said. An association will finalize its budget for the upcoming year toward the end of their current year. Then Strussione also recommended that the association review the budget 4-6 months after the start of the new year to compare actual expenses to their projections.

What is the association's operating fund?

It's everything an association needs to bring in and pay out in their monthly expenses. Your operating fund, at the end of the year, is like the retained earnings in the business world. It's the end profit or loss of all the operating years of income and expenses. The goal as a non-profit association is to bring it to zero every year.

Does the association's accountant typically review the budget prior to its being approved by the board? "We typically see it after," she said. Although, sometimes boards will consult with their accountants prior to approving their budgets to see if they have any recommendations. "It's a good idea," she said, "because your auditors sometimes catch mistakes that the board makes."

Financial Statements

What are an association's annual reporting requirements for financial statements? According to Strussione, under the AICPA rules, the association's accountant is required to follow the Codification Code for financial statement presentations for condominium associations. The now mandated methods were formerly guidelines, but starting in 2009, they were placed under the AICPA Codification Code. "If you are a CPA and you belong to the AICPA, you are mandated to report using the Codification Code," she said. She warned if you use a CPA firm that is not familiar with accounting for common interest realty associations (CIRA), their reporting will most-likely not conform with the rules on financial statement presentation for a condominium association.

Unlike a budget, which is the board of directors' projection of income and expenses for the fiscal year, the financial statement is the actual report of the association's income and expenses. The board and manager should analyze this report when preparing the budget for the next year and look for items they think may be variable in the upcoming year. For example, if the association knows that water rates will be going up in their city or municipality, they should incorporate the increase into their upcoming budget. Another variable expense is insurance. Additionally, the association should do a physical inspection of their property to see if there are any big projects that may need to be tackled in the upcoming year. "They should do physical inspection reports," said Strussione. "You need to pay attention to that and see if they need to be incorporated into the budget."

Association Taxes

What types of tax returns does an association file? The two types of tax returns a condominium association is allowed to file, on the federal level, are Form 1120, which is the tax return for corporations, including condominium associations, or Form 1120-H, which is the tax return mandated for homeowners associations (HOAs) and which can also be used by condominium associations.

The calculation of income for both of these types of returns is the same. For each you must separate the membership income from non-membership income, because membership income is not subject to tax. The membership income is the income received from all regular members, such as assessments and late charges. The taxable income is the non-membership income. This would include things like income from clubhouse rental, interest income, dividends and capital gains.

The calculation for the expenses is the same on both types of returns as well. You can deduct a percentage of your management fees, accounting fees and administrative costs.

So what are the differences between filing the 1120 versus the 1120-H? "The difference is that on Form 1120, the net taxable income is subject to a graduated tax starting at 15 percent. Also, if there is a net-operating loss, associations can carry that over for up to 20 years. For Form 1120-H, the taxable income calculation is the same, but the tax rate is a 30 percent flat tax after a $100 allowed deduction." said Strussione.

In Michigan, as well as some other states, if associations file Form 1120-H, they do not need to also file a corporate state tax return. While this seems like an incentive to file the 1120-H, Strussione said there is no advantage to doing this. "When you look at it, Michigan state tax is only 6 percent. So you're better off filing the federal at 15 percent and the state at 6 percent — it's only 21 percent, and you get the loss carry forward versus if you file the 1120-H, you pay a flat 30 percent," she said. She also said this would be a state-by-state decision, since every state has a different way of calculating their state taxes as well as different tax percentages.

So why would anyone ever file the 1120-H? Certain associations that are true HOAs are mandated by the government to file the 1120-H. So

👉 IRS Revenue Rule 70-604

Each fiscal year a condominium association has excess assessments over expenses, a net profit, or excess expenses over assessments, a net loss. The Internal Revenue Rule 70-604 states that if there are excess assessments over expenses these monies must be returned to the co-owners or applied to the following year's assessments in order for them not to be taxable to the corporation.

A condominium association is subject to tax under the Federal IRS rules even though it is incorporated as a non-profit in the State of Michigan. A meeting should be held each year where a responsible party, board of directors, or vote by election decides whether to have any excess paid back to themselves or to have the excess applied against the following year's assessments. To apply to the next year, Strussione suggests that they prepare the subsequent year's budget and add an income line "carry forward from IRS Rev-Rule 70-604" for a line item amount. Then, in order to not throw off the budget, include a separate expense line called "contingent expenses" for the same amount. This amount is, at best, an estimate, as the actual amount is usually not known at the time of budget preparation. She also suggests that the board of directors make the vote and document the board of directors' minutes stating that they have elected to carry forward any excess assessments per IRS Rev-Rule 70-604. "For our condominium association tax clients, we include a separate line on the attachment page to the Form 1120-Corporate Tax Return stating that 'per IRS Rev-Rule 70-604 the excess will be carried forward,' and we show the calculation," Strussione explained.

The IRS code section does not state who must make the election. Our firm contacted the IRS on January 31, 2002 and documented that it doesn't matter who makes the election as long as it is a party responsible to make decisions for the corporation. Therefore, the board of directors can make the election and avoid having to take it to all residents for a vote.

— Linda R. Strussione, CPA

condominium associations can choose to file the 1120 rather than the 1120-H, but HOAs do not have this choice. "In the eyes of the IRS, if you're a condominium association, on an annual election basis, you get to elect which of the two forms you file," she said.

Association Audits — New Rules in Michigan

There was a recent amendment to the Michigan Condominium Act that affects the requirements for community association audits. The new State of Michigan requirements are in effect for associations with fiscal years starting after January 14, 2014. The change affects all condominium associations of co-owners with annual revenues greater than $20,000. The amendment specifies that these associations need to have an audit or review of their records and financial statements performed by a certified public accountant (CPA) on an annual basis. In the past, associations could do a compilation of their records. This is no longer allowed because it is mandated that an audit or review is needed.

Such associations have an option to opt-out of these new audit and review requirements, but they must do it on an annual basis. In order to opt-out, they need to have a majority vote of the membership — that is all co-owners — declaring that they want to opt out. The majority vote needs be repeated on an annual basis, and done in accordance with the association's bylaws.

"If they don't have an election to opt-out, then they need to have an audit or review engagement performed," said Strussione.

If an association successfully votes to opt-out of the audit or review requirement, they can then do a compilation and tax return.

Strussione said that this amendment is the biggest change in the State of Michigan's condominium association accounting in over 30 years.

What is a compilation?

This is a report of the association's records as prepared by the association, without being audited or reviewed by a CPA. Associations that are not mandated to have an audit or review could give a compilation of their records to their accountant to use in preparing their tax return. The accountant doing a tax return from a compilation does not check the association's records. They prepare the association's return based on the compilation — that is, the figures reported to the accountant by the association.

Recognizing and Preventing Fraud

How can associations protect themselves from fraud? The most common scenario of theft of association funds occurs when an association allows their bookkeeper to physically make deposits of the association's money and also approve invoices and pay bills. "There is no division of duty," said Strussione. "That is the biggest threat of fraud to an association.

Another common threat is when a board allows for only one signer on a bank account. "They just allow one board member to be the signer on a reserve savings, certificate of deposit, or checking account, without requiring two signatures," said Strussione. This gives the signer the opportunity to commit fraud. "With a second signer on a bank account you would need to have two people in cahoots together if you're paying fictitious bills. It could happen, but it's less likely if you have more than one signer on the bank account," she said. Strussione recommended having either two board members as signers, or a board member and someone from the association's management company.

What are some of the warning signs that theft or fraud is occurring? One warning sign is when a board member who is the only signer on the bank account is having the association's bank statements mailed directly to their home. "That is a fraud indicator right there," said Strussione. "They're controlling the bank account as the only signer and no one else is privy to those bank statements. That's your biggest problem right there."

Another indicator is if you have board members that have altered their lifestyle. "You see them purchasing or living beyond their means," she said. She also warns about board members who express they have financial concerns of their own or for a family member. A person experiencing a desperate financial situation could be a potential threat for committing fraud against the association.

Selecting an Accounting Firm

Strussione said that the most important thing to look for in an accounting firm is if they are a member of the Michigan Association of Certified Public Accountants (MICPA) and the AICPA. If the firm is a member of the AICPA, they're mandated to belong to the Peer Review Program. So the association needs to find out if the firm is a part of the AICPA, and if they are, that the CPA firm is having their mandated Peer

Reviews done every three years. Also, what types of reports are they getting on these Peer Reviews?

If an association is bringing someone in to perform an audit, Strussione strongly recommended asking if they are in compliance with the AICPA's Peer Review Program. She said further that you should ask to see a copy of their latest Peer Review acceptance letter. Strussione stressed that, in Michigan, CPAs are not allowed to be performing audits or reviews unless they're part of the Peer Review Program.

She explained further what the AICPA's Peer Review program consists of. Based on the size of the firm, they can either self-select another CPA firm to come and perform the peer review, or they can turn their records in to the state to do the peer review. Small companies, such as those with one CPA, are allowed to submit their own records to the State of Michigan and the state performs the Peer Review. Medium or large sized firms need to have an outside accounting firm come in and audit their records to make sure the CPA firm is complying with the AICPA's rules. Firms are reviewed on how they prepare financial statements, how they audit, how they document their work papers, if they're keeping up with the standards of the AICPA, if they're complying with the government's rules on how to do financial statements for condominium associations, and more. "It's a really big thing," she said.

Strussione also recommended asking about the firm's expertise in working with condominium associations. Find out if they are preparing financials using the Codification Code for Common Interest Realty Associations (CIRA). Ask what position they take in preparing a financial statement. Do they take the position of filing Form 1120 for a corporation and take advantage of net operating loss rules, or do they file a simple 1120-H Homeowner Association Tax Return? What are the qualifications of the people who will be doing the association's audit? What continuing education classes do the firm's accountants take to keep up their CPA licenses? Are any of those classes taken for government reporting, or working with condominium and homeowner associations? What type of continuing education keeps them up-to-date with condominium associations? "These are all pretty important questions," said Strussione.

How Will an Association Be Billed for Their Accounting Services?

The cost for accounting services will vary based on several factors, such as if an association has a lot of reserve activity, if they're bringing in monthly dues versus annual dues, and the size of the association in terms of the number of cash receipts and cash disbursements per month. "Those items are what indicates to a CPA firm what to charge an association," said Strussione.

She also said the majority of associations are billed on a fixed fee. "They pay one price to do the job," she said. Other associations, however, are billed per diem because the activity in their situation varies from year to year. Some years they are billed more, and some less, based on what is going on. "Some of the condos are so complex that CPAs just charge by the hour to do the job," she said. The hourly bills should have detail outlining how many hours of staff time and how many hours of partner time are included in the billing.

One last bit of advice Strussione gives is not to select a firm solely based on price. "You need to see if people are really checking your records," she said.

12

Financial Management, Nuts & Bolts on Budgeting and Financial Warning Signs

Financial management is perhaps one of the most critical facets of a homeowners association. Financial transactions factor into day-to-day interactions in an HOA, with residents paying dues and vendors providing goods and services. The complexities of an HOA, however, demand a business-like approach to financial matters in order to provide a well-functioning environment for all involved. Budgets, therefore, become essential to success.

How does an association diagram a budget? What can the association do to limit surprises in a budget? How do reserve studies factor in? What are the different types of budgets? Creating a sound budget and adhering to it for the fiscal year for the association is very important. Tom Engblom, CMCA, AMS, PCAM, VP/Regional Account Executive at Mutual of Omaha Bank provided us with an explanation of the budget process.

According to Engblom, "A budget is a roadmap that provides an estimate of a community's revenue, expenses and reserves. It provides an avenue for a community to plan activities, goals, maintenance, repairs, reserves, determine assessments, and minimize the unexpected." While the necessity of an association budget may seem clear, the process itself can be quite complex. Engblom stated that an association should first consider the legal requirements for a budget in their state. Refer to state statutes as well as the governing documents of your association as your guidelines. "Every community association must have a budget. It is required at various levels of the law and in the governing documents," Engblom said. He added that local laws may require a budget, whether for insurance, emergency, life safety, etc. All associations must conform to IRS rules, and mortgage institutions may set requirements that a community will need to meet as well. Additionally, budgets manadate the procedures to determine the applicable requirement for reserves.

Once the legal necessity of a budget has been established, how must your association proceed? From there, your association may take into account the needs and desires of homeowners. What services do they require on a daily, weekly, monthly and yearly basis? Which do they expect? Engblom also noted that associations should not simply aim for a net profit or loss. Don't simply set a budget including all known expenses (i.e. routine maintenance, electricity, water, etc.). The budget will also need to account for and include unexpected expenses. If, for example, a natural disaster occurs, your association will need to be prepared. Ideally, a budget will limit the impact of financial surprises. Within a budget there is a chart of accounts, which is an organized list of the numbers of the association, categorzied showing each item being budgeted for. This is detailed in the previous chapter on association accounting under the heading "Organizing Budgets."

Assembling the Budget

When is the budget due? This depends on the association and is generally contained within the bylaws. Typically, budgets are done either

> Income - Expenses = Net Operating Income (NOI)
> Extra money goes into reserves.

by calendar year or fiscal year. Most do them by calendar year, Engblom noted. The association's manager typically puts the budget together. A budget committee, headed by the board treasurer, can be formed by board resolution to come up with the nuances in the budget. This is an ongoing, standing committee. Engblom again underscored that an association should not just budget for money it expects or does not have. As an example, Engblom said, "You shouldn't necessarily be budgeting for fines and late fees." If income is not expected, don't budget as if it is.

There are two components of a budget: revenue and expenses.
- *Revenue:* assessments (which Engblom noted is the only component of value that an association has), excluding miscellaneous income of late fees, fines, move ins and move outs, etc.
- *Expenses:* operating expenses (i.e. maintenance, utilities, administrative, management, insurance, copying, printing, Internet, etc.)

Furthermore, two components are affiliated with each budget line as to whether it is mandatory or discretionary. Mandatory expenses are things such as insurance and utilities. These are expenses the association is obligated to cover, as opposed to discretionary items such as pool furniture, a community newsletter or the expectation of an individual unit owner.

There are also two types of budgets:
- *Zero base:* In this type of budget all line items are set to zero. Therefore, all line items must be justified, rather than assuming a base line from the prior year. This assures that every line item is necessary and reduces the fluff within the budget. This zero base approach requires every line item to be calculated accordingly (i.e. utilities) based on usage.
- *Historical trend:* In this type of budget an association uses the historical data from budgets past, then reviews its past history to determine what the increase or decrease in expenses will be for the next year. As an example, Engblom said, "To increase the percentage, you can look at two years ago. You spent 17%, and then this year you spent 19%. So you know to increase 2% again for the next year." Typically the budget has numerous line items that have inaccurate numbers in those accounts.

There are three (3) types of accounting methods to be used within a budget as follows:
1. *Cash method:* Using this method, the association will collect money and pay it out as invoices are received. A great comparsion would be one's personal checkbook.
2. *Accrual* is based on when income is earned (or billed), and when expense are incurred. Income and expenses are accounted for outside of when the actual cash comes in or goes out.
3. *Modified cash* also know as *modified accrual* is the most complicated method for accounting, but also the best. It records income and expense on a cash basis with some on a accrual basis.

As mentioned earlier, the association can take into account the needs of the homeowners. Budget line items are determined to be either mandatory or discretionary. Mandatory line items are a need or an obligation, such as water, insurance, or taxes. Discretionary line items are a desire or expectation, such as a pool, playground, or golf course. The discretionary items can be ranked based on the desires of the homeowners, but mandatory items must always be budgeted for.

How the Reserve Study Relates to the Budget

Reserve studies themselves are detailed in Chapter 8, but here is an overview of the studies and how they are utilized within the framework of budget creation. Once revenue and expenses are established, the association has the so-called bottom line of the budget. Engblom advised that reserves are taken out at this point. Reserve studies serve as a resource for capital expenditures that would be in the the future of the association. The reserve study consist of two components including a physical inspection and a financial inspection. "Reserve funds are set aside for the future, for replacement of major components of an association," Engblom said, "and reserve studies should be updated every three to five years." They may be required by a state statute, regulations, mortgagees, or the association's own governing documents. The Federal Housing Administration suggests setting aside 10% of the total budget for reserves.

Funding for reserves consist of 4 aspect as follows:
1. *Statutory* — required by state or federal agencies

2. *Fund Safety* — Maintain in FDIC insured accounts.
3. *Liquidy* — Don't have all funds in certificate. Have some cash on hand for emergencies.
4. *Yield* — The return on investments

Reserve studies generally include capital improvements and major improvements. Capital improvements include existing entities that must be replaced, such as a roof, siding or playground equipment. Reserve studies set money aside for the future, anticipating that something will need to be replaced or repaired. Engblom noted that the amount of money set aside can be judged from the useful life of the structure in question. As an example, "A roof has a 30 year useful life, but because of weather or the like, it may need to be replaced sooner or later. Reserve studies plan for putting aside money for these sort of things," Engblom said.

Major improvements, on the other hand, include the addition of something new to the association, such as a clubhouse, pool, or golf course. These improvements are not being maintained, as with a capital improvement, but rather they are being constructed for the first time.

Engblom pointed out some of the benefits of using a reserve study: meets legal and fiduciary professional requirements, provides for planned replacement of major components, minimizes the need for special assessments, enhances the resale value of units, equalizes new and old, reduces personal liability from financial mismanagement, prioritizes a business plan for repairs, acts as a communication tool for the owners, can reveal maintenance issues that you haven't seen, saves planning time, reveals un-budgeted items

He also mentioned some of the drawbacks of a reserve study: underfunding resulting in the need for a bank loan, deferred maintenance, overfunding, board member liability and possible loss of directors & officers liability insurance.

In relation to a budget, a reserve study can most importantly determine what has not yet been budgeted for. It can provide an association with a more thorough road map for the what-if scenarios and help secure an association's future.

Financial Warning Signs

Engblom noted that there are certain financial warning signs that associations must look out for. As mentioned before, reserves are a necessary aspect to the life of the association. If replacement reserves not set aside, the association may have a problem. Why weren't they set aside from the rest of the budget? This underscores the necessity of having a transparent budgeting process and making sure that all expenses are accounted for, even those hypotheticals that are backed up by a reserve fund.

Further financial warning signs include increased overdue assessments (delinqucies) or an increase in what the association owes. Engblom advised that associations should look for significant differences between budget figures. Has the budget for a certain line item suddenly propelled upward? Additional signs of financial mismanagement include when members' equity is less than one to three months of the operating expense. Maintaining control of the finances within the budget and reserve fund will provide an avenue of unpexepected hurdles for the board and the homeowners in preventing a financial impact in the form of a special assessment.

In addition, having control of your financial reports will provide a means of best practices for procedures relating to accounts receivable or accounts payable. In the global aspect for the association it can help discourage dishonest behavior within the association that may result in embezzlement, fraud or theft.

13

Calculating Association Assessments

Assessments are a common conduit of condominium and homeowners associations, as an intricate component in providing income for the operating budget and funding reserves for future community expenditures. Thomas Engblom, CMCA, AMS, PCAM, VP/Regional Account Executive at Mutual of Omaha Bank, detailed for us what assessments are, how they are calculated, and how special assessments factor in. Of course, in order to keep your association running well, you must understand assessments and their purpose in aiding financial stability.

"Assessments are the proportionate shares of the expenses to maintain the property of the association," Engblom said. Assessments are sometimes called maintenance fees or dues. How are assessments calculated? "They're typically calculated on a percentage of ownership — which never changes for each co-owner. However, there can be a change in the monetary amount of the fees, but it will always be based on that owner's same percentage of ownership." Assessments are usually calculated in the initial phase of the association by the developer. "The developer creates a mathematical formula based on the cost of maintaining the new association," he said. Engblom noted that as the association ages, logically, additional

> **☞ Calculating Percentage of Ownership**
>
> Percentage of ownership always equals 100% when all units are combined. Engblom's example: "If all the units were the same size, and you only have 10 of them, each unit would have 10% of ownership. If you have 1,000 units, the percentage decreases as the percentage sum must always equal 100%. The equation to calculate the percentage is based on square footage and/or location of the unit. Henceforth, square footage of units will change the percentage of assessments depending on their percentage of ownership."

maintence is required thus increasing the association's fees. In Chapter 6, changes in fees after the developer leaves the community are discussed.

Each owner's percentage of ownership can always be found in the association's governing documents.

What could cause assessments to be higher in one association as opposed to another, even though all variables and amenities are equal? Assessments are quite dependent on the actions and professionalism of the board and management. If those running the community are educated in association managment, they will have the knowledge to provide a budgetary structure that will maintain the association in its daily operations, as well as building proper reserves for the future. However, it is also important that those running the community adhere to their fiduciary duties, and always act in the best interest of the association. Problems can occur when an association's governing body is only concerned with the political advantages of maintaining low fees. In the most drastic situations, some board members, knowing they want to sell their units in a few years, can make the community seem attractive to potential buyers by keeping fees artificially low while not putting any funds in reserves. Such a community would eventually come in for a crash landing — specifically, needing to special assess the unit owners and/or obtain a bank loan for capital improvements as they became necessary, or otherwise causing the physical association to deteriorate.

Engblom pointed out other factors which affect fees among different communities. "If you're going to buy in an association with a pool, it will cost you considerably more to live there compared to a association without a pool. A pool will require maintenance, repairs, chemicals, furniture, attendants and more. Communities with pools also have an increased insurance cost over those without. Assessments are the sheer cost of living for the association — what it costs to maintain the common areas of that community. Comparatively, owners of single homes outside of a community incur costs to run and maintain their homes and properties. In a community, these similar costs are multiplied by the number of units for those similar needs."

When special assessments or fee increases are necessary, associations cannot randomly calculate assessments based on the whim of the board. The assessment or increase must be made within the parameters of the governing documents and specific state statutory requirements.

Collecting Assessments

Collection procedures for delinquent unit owners are detailed in Chapter 2, however here, Engblom outlined the methods and importance of collecting regular dues, and how to evaluate the health of an association based on its delinquency rate.

Assessments are a financial obligation to the community association during a given period of time, which is usually broken down into payments, such as monthly, quarterly, etc., unless a long-term special assessment is manadated. "Assessments are paid pursuant to the governing documents of the association. They're mandatory, so residents are obligated to pay them," Engblom explained. Presently, numerous methods for payment are available — check, ACH (automatic debit), online payments through an association or bank website and credit card.

Every association should have a formal collection policy and take the time to educate owners about the consequences of delinquency. Associations should avoid discriminatory actions against delinquent account holders. "You should have a procedure and protocol — rule or regulation," Engblom said. Board members can establish these procedures utilizing the business judgement rule, he added. Not only can this improve relationships and communication between the board and the residents, but it can also help ensure that assessments and monthly fees are paid on time. Further, collections are crucial to maintaining necessary cash-flow and to reducing loss of payments from owners. "The bottom line," Engblom said, "is that a collection policy keeps owners informed, provides a guide for the manager, and enforces a written policy."

Since assessments make up the major portion of an association's income, it is crucial that they are paid by the unit owners. However, most associations have at least some delinquent owner accounts. Engblom delineated the delinquency rates and how they should be evaluated:

0-3%	good delinquency rate
4-5%	reasonable delinquency rate
6-10%	declining delinquency rate
10%	horrendous delinquency rate
Over 10%	very bad delinquency rate

Engblom also noted that for association loans, delinquency rates must be less than 10%.

Special Assessments

Special assessments, in addition to regular dues, sometimes constitute part of an HOA's income. Special assessments generally make up for

> ### 👉 An Example of How Special Assessments Are Implemented
>
> "Let me give you a situation," said Engblom. "One of the properties that I own as an investment property had a swimming pool. The swimming pool was used by hardly anyone, and it was costing the association approximately $35,000 each year. There were numerous problems with the pool. Suddenly, the association was going to need to spend $60,000 obtaining proper licensing from the state. The board said, 'Well, we're not going to waste that kind of money. For $70,000, we're going to fill that pool in.' The community decided to put a park in place of the pool area, thereby deleting the pool expense from the budget forever! This resulted in a three year pack back for the association. The association manadated a special assessment — a one-time charge paid either in a lump sum within two months, or monthly for five years at $50 per month, including interest as a result of the funding by the association."

expenses that cannot be covered by the budget, either because operating expenses exceeded the budget, a natural disaster or similar situation occurred, a special project began, or too many residents were delinquent in their dues. Reserve funds, as noted in Chapters 8 and 12, alleviate some of the pressure of unexpected expenses. Special assessments pick up any monetary gaps not covered by reserves or the budget. Engblom said, "They are a one-time fee or charge." They are not charged regularly as plain assessments are, although they can be collected on a similar schedule (i.e. monthly, quarterly, or annually). The dollar amount of the special assessment each unit owner pays similarly depends on their percentage of ownership.

A special assessment is typically voted on by an association's board for an item or project that was not voted on previously during the annual budget planning. "It's all driven by what the state requirements are, but in theory, the board approves the budget or special assessment. The board communicates the information, allowing the unit owners to review or discuss it at a subsequent special meeting for the purpose of the special assessment. The board always has the power to initiate the budget or the special assessment, however, depending on the governing documents or state statute, final approval may be contingent upon a vote of the the unit owners. Furthermore, some states allow unit owners to petition the board of director's decisions thereby repealing an action of the board while other states don't allow that option.

14

Association Board Meetings

Board meetings personify the community aspect of running a homeowner or condominium association. The act of meeting in person to discuss the wants and needs of the community, to problem solve, and to plan for the future of the association heightens the importance of conducting efficient, informative and inclusive meetings. Thomas Engblom, CMCA, AMS, PCAM, VP/Regional Account Executive at Mutual of Omaha Bank provided us with a guide to board meetings, including scheduling, conduct and communication with board members and residents.

"Initially, an association must determine the location and frequency of its board meetings pursuant to the association's governing documents. The governing documents and/or the state are going to mandate how often meetings should be held, and it depends on the type of the association," Engblom said. If you have a smaller association, does the board need to meet every month? Absolutely not. However, a larger association (or its committees), depending on the number of units, projects and status of the board, could meet bi-monthly, monthly, or quarterly. As for location, select a professional environment, even if the location is not necessarily within the association's boundaries. "You don't want to meet at a bar, restaurant, or someone's home. You should meet at a library or an office because it will increase the productivity of the meeting as well as improve on the atmosphere for those that are attending," Engblom said.

In addition, meetings with established times and locations can be designated as either closed or open. Open meetings, as implied, allow for unit owners to attend in addition to the board members. Open meetings are suitable for numerous aspects that pertain to the management of the association or the administrative functionality. Closed meetings typically follow a different format relating to litigation, violations, fee delinquencies or employee-related matters," Engblom said. Inasmuch, budget meetings should be open, as the board should be transparent with unit owners on issues pertaining to the fiscal aspects of the association.

The number of board members required to be present at meetings is determined within the association documents and depends on the parameters of the association, originated by the developer.

Property managers and supervisors typically attend meetings in addition to board members and unit owners, though their attendance depends more on the size of the property. Typically, managers will attend all of the meetings of larger associations but won't attend all of the meetings of certain smaller associations due to financial constraints. "Regardless of the size of the association, all boards should establish and follow the business judgment rule, acting within their fiduciary duties, in order to avoid potential litigation," Engblom said.

The board can notify the association of an upcoming meeting in a myriad of ways. Engblom noted that the old-fashioned way involved posting notices in a conspicuous location or sending them by mail. In addition, notices could be included with the monthly statements, payment coupon books, or posted on the association website, among other options. If the board has a set schedule (i.e. they meet the first Monday of every month), they can simply post ongoing notices to inform owners of that, rather than sending out new notices for each meeting. "However, a special meeting must meet the proper requirements for giving notice, regardless of what purpose the meeting was called for," Engblom said.

With regard to agendas and meeting minutes, agendas can be sent out in advance, although the board may not know the full extent of the agenda until just prior to the meeting, which would require the agenda to be updated. The course of action with the agenda and minutes, however, can vary from association to association. "It depends on the environment of the association. I would not send out the agenda before the meeting, but I would hand out the agenda the night of the meeting," Engblom noted.

Board meetings should follow Robert's Rules of Order, which specify what should be recorded in meeting minutes, as well as the manner in which the meeting is conducted. Motions are made, then seconded and approved by board members. The meeting minutes record action items only, rather than each point brought up by attendees. Meetings should start on time and end on time, and discussions should be kept on track in order to maintain efficiency. Stay on track by following the agenda and utilizing time parameters. Questions can be taken from residents at the end of the meeting during an open forum.

As for recording meetings, whether by video or audio, the ability to do this, again, depends on the association's declaration and the state in which the association is located.

Residents or board members who are unruly at meetings will stymie the board — possibly arguing over how to conduct business. Engblom advised that if residents become unruly, require a point of order. If an unruly individual continues to disturb the meeting, request that he or she leaves. If that person refuses, either contact the authorities or adjourn the meeting and reconvene at a later time.

Establishing the community and leadership aspects of the board are important factors in the success of the association. The board is responsible for making important decisions for the association, including establishing the budget and assessments. Its decisions, and the process used in making them, affect the governance of the association as well as its sense of community. This underscores the importance of effective meetings in maintaining professional yet transparent leadership in your association.

15

Working With and Motivating Volunteers on the Board and Committees

Motivating volunteers is a lot different than motivating co-workers or employees in a business environment. In the case of professional employment, monetary compensation, and the hopeful possibility of increasing one's compensation, are driving forces in motivation. Fear also plays a role in motivating those in a work environment. If employees are not pulling their weight, there's always a risk that they will be reprimanded, or possibly terminated. Professionals who slack off run the risk of falling behind their peers and competitors, thereby losing credibility and possibly decreasing earning potential. Money and the fear of losing money are possibly the most powerful motivators out there.

So what are the techniques for motivating those who are not directly gaining monetary compensation? In particular, what motivates the HOA or condo association board member or volunteer? What is to be done about a volunteer condo or HOA board or committee member who is not participating at an acceptable level? This is where the art of motivating volunteers comes in.

Understand the Reasons People Volunteer

First, one needs to consider some of the many reasons individuals volunteer for these positions:

1. The person is bored and looking for a way to keep busy.
2. The person feels that there is no one else willing or able to do the job.
3. The person is lonely and looking for human interaction.
4. The person has a desire to be proactive in maintaining or improving their community for the reason of maintaining or increasing their property's value.
5. The person is asked and can't say no.
6. The person is not happy with how the community is running and has a better way of doing things.
7. The person has the need to be in control of a group of other people and finds the opportunity by serving on their association's board.

Now before determining that lack of overall motivation is the culprit in an under performing volunteer, consider why that individual may have joined the board in the first place. Then ask yourself if this person is being given the opportunity to serve on the board or committee in a way that is meaningful to them? Not to misunderstand, the board is not there to give volunteers jobs solely based on what each particular volunteer's desires are. But bearing in mind one's reason for volunteering can give a leader insight into how to best place volunteers in positions, and motivate them to perform to their best ability in those positions. The two factors go hand-in-hand.

Additionally, a good first step is to make sure volunteers are given tasks and responsibilities which they are qualified and able to do. Volunteers on a homeowner board will learn many things along the way during their terms. However, keep in mind that many people feel comfortable volunteering for responsibilities they are not even close to being qualified for. If someone is new to the board, and has no prior similar experience, a great way to keep them on a positive and productive path is to have them work in tandem with another more experienced board member. This way the leaders will be able to determine the individual's strengths and abilities.

Tap into those, as you will get the most out of each volunteer by playing on their strengths. Individuals given tasks they have no qualifications or aptitude to do will likely flounder and possibly fail. That person will likely leave the board at the end of their term without making any meaningful contribution.

To give an example, let's say hypothetical HOA resident "Betty" joins the board. She is a retired kindergarten teacher who recently moved to the community from another area. She feels she has the time to serve her community, as well as a desire to meet other residents and board members for social reasons. This is her first experience living in an HOA, and she is completely unfamiliar with the issues involved. Since Betty is joining the board, at least partially, for social reasons, she will be very motivated if given encouragement and positive feedback from those she interacts with in her position. As mentioned above, since she has no HOA experience, the best approach, for the first few months at least, is to pair her with hypothetical "Bob," a seasoned board member with three years under his belt. Bob is board secretary, and one of his many jobs is recruiting members to serve on the community's social committee, as well as running that committee. Bob can parlay his experience on the board to Betty, so she can help recruit for, and eventually take over managing this committee. Betty's experience working at a school, being a former a teacher with experience planning activities and working with other faculty and administration, gives her the perfect skills to do this job. Additionally, her desire to meet others in the community will hereby be fulfilled. I see Betty thriving in this job.

On the other hand, let's say Betty joins the board and is given the job of working with the architectural committee. She is still being paired with an experienced board member to begin with, however the work here is a bit different. Betty is now faced with the task of doling out fines for architectural violations, deciding whether or not to approve the proposed projects of residents, and holding up construction, possibly adding cost to repairs and holding up landscaping projects to the point where it's too late in the season to even do them. At this point Betty has had so many negative interactions with residents that she has no hope of making friends. She is counting the days until her term is up, and is even considering moving!

So the architectural committee sounds like a lousy job, right? Well let's say hypothetical "Jake" fits the description of person number 7 in the list above. Serving on the architectural committee sounds like a dream come true for Jake. He will be given the opportunity to make and enforce the rules of this committee. He likes being in charge, and this position provides him the perfect scenario to fulfill this desire. Jake will thrive in this position. Alternatively, if Jake was placed on the social committee, he may not be very effective. His need to control people would most likely have a the effect of simply repelling people. His tendency to control can make him difficult to work with, and since participating in social events is optional, the committee would probably have a very low level of participation.

So these examples show how there is a purpose for every type of person. The main thing to remember, if you want to get the most out of those willing to serve, is that you need to match skills as well as the individual's reason for volunteering with whatever you assign them to do. If you do this, you will have a highly energized group of volunteers.

Have Realistic Expectations

Many people in leadership positions expect the same level of commitment to the association that they themselves are willing to offer. That's just not feasible and it's also not fair. It is up to the leaders of the association to determine a realistic level of commitment for each volunteer they recruit.

Not everyone cares about the association to the same extent, but that doesn't mean less-committed individuals can't be utilized in a very valuable way for the community. Additionally, it's my opinion that even a little participation, from a greater number of people, will foster fuller caring and commitment to your community. This can translate into fewer violations and delinquencies, greater participation at elections, and just a better community overall. Some people want to volunteer, but can only do so, or only want to do so, in a limited capacity. The fact that they want to do something is the important factor here. And those in charge should take advantage of this. There are many small jobs that need to be done, and the more volunteers that are welcomed into the fold, the more the community will be cared for.

Let's take hypothetical "Cindy" for example. She understands there is a lot involved in running the community. She attends some resident meetings when she is able to. She has been asked to serve on the board, but declined for numerous reasons. She doesn't want to with the hassle of needing to attend monthly meetings, and doesn't want to be bothered with resident issues. She also has an elderly mother she is caring for, in addition to her three children, and has limited free time. After declining to serve on the board, Cindy learned the community is looking for articles for its quarterly newsletter. Cindy enjoys writing, and since this can be done on her own time, would like to be involved with the community in the capacity of providing the quarterly gardening article for the newsletter. This helps the community, as well as providing Cindy with a meaningful position, which she is able to do and enjoys doing. Her position enriches the community, as well as her experience living in it. She is approached by residents, but in the capacity that they are enjoying her column and sharing information about the topic of gardening. This is a win/win for this volunteer.

Let's take hypothetical board member "Larry" as another example. In his five years on the board there was an issue every year at election time. Someone was needed to help facilitate the election, and no one was ever chosen to do so. So every year the board was not able to conduct the annual election meeting in the manner which they would like, as they were busy with residents who only come out once a year with complaints and a complete lack of knowledge about the voting procedure. This year, Larry decides to recruit three individuals to help facilitate the election. These individuals, hypothetical "Renee," "Joe," and "Lucy," are more than happy to be asked. They are already looking forward to helping out next year. None of these three are interested in doing any other volunteer work for the association, but they are more than happy to have the annual election to look forward to every year. It makes them feel connected to the community, and that they are making a meaningful and useful contribution. The board benefits, as they have these individuals to rely on every year at election time. This is another win/win in utilizing less-involved volunteers.

A serious problem is when a volunteer is holding an important position on the board, and does not have a level of commitment required for this. Board members have an obligation to fulfill their fiduciary duties, and this means 100% commitment to running the community. Maybe this person was fine going into the job, and subsequently suffered a personal hardship, such as family illness or job loss, and now they are like a non-existent board member. In these situations, leaders need to recognize lack of motivation is not the root of this problem. These people had the best of intentions when they joined the board, yet their personal circumstances have made it impossible for them to fulfill their roles. Another board member, or the president should step in here. Communicate with the individual to see if they need a break, would like to stay on regardless of their issue, or if they would prefer to resign their position so someone else can come in. Oftentimes troubled individuals will be glad you asked them, as it can be difficult for someone who has made such an important commitment to admit they may not be able to fulfill it. Approaching these individuals gives them the opportunity to save face, and serves another purpose of leaving the door open for them, if they do decide to step back, to return to their position when ready. After all, this person was once a highly productive and dedicated volunteer, and so it's possible they will be again.

Diffuse the Bullies

Refer to number 6 in the list at the beginning of this chapter. It's amazing a person like this was elected to the board in the first place, however they are motivated — they want to get things done. They are also very knowledgeable, which is a huge asset to the board. This person is ready, willing and able to jump right into a top board position. The problem is that they think the only right way to do things is their way. The only vision for the community is theirs, and it does not mesh with the current path of the community's governance. Someone like this can kill the motivation of other board members and volunteers. So what can be done? Aside from suffering a coup d'etat brought on by one member, the board should hear this individual out. The entire board should have a conversation about what his or her issues and ideas are. Compare them with the board's current plans and genuinely consider the pros and cons of making the changes in accordance with what this individual is proposing. If the person truly is simply a bully who just needs to be heard, this conversation should suffice in bringing him on board with the current activities of the association. Although time-consuming, or wasting as the case may or may not be, communities are run by owner-controlled boards, so this is a necessary conversation to have. It's part of the community aspect of the HOA or condo association. Look at the conversation as a reminder to the veteran board members that other ways and opinions do exist. Who knows? The board could actually benefit from changing the way certain things are done. This is part of the reason why it's important to have a certain level of board member turnover. One complaint in communities is that certain boards just seem to stay on forever, and nothing ever changes. This could be okay — but let's face it, there is always the possibility for improvement in every situation.

Alternatively, if this board member continually second-guesses every decision and is constantly at odds with the rest of the group, the community will suffer. All members of the board, even if they don't agree on everything, must be able to work together in order to keep the community moving on solid ground. Compromises often need to be made, however if a board member is unable to work with the group and impedes the functioning of the board, they are not fulfilling their fiduciary duty to act in the best interest of the community. Additionally, if the individual is belligerent and prevents the board from doing its job, the association's attorney may need to get involved in order to remove the individual. And it goes without saying that, just as in a professional work environment, those working as volunteers on the board should not be subjected to abusive behavior from a fellow board member.

Beware of the Word Yes

Be on the lookout for this special breed of person described in number 5 in the list at the beginning of this chapter. They just can't say the simple word "no." When asking this person to do something, bear in mind their inability to say "no" may be the only reason they will accept responsibility for the task you ask them to do. It is very, very tempting to ask for the help of these individuals — you will not be rejected! But as with any volunteers, don't ask these people to do things you know they won't be able to do. Otherwise, you may be surprised that even though they say "yes" to doing a task, it may or may not get done.

Let's look at the example of hypothetical "Jennie." She is currently on the board of her church, a girl scout leader, on the town's school board, a hospital volunteer, room mother of her child's class at school, coach for her other child's softball team and a docent at a local museum. Just knowing all this about Jennie should tell you that she probably has a little problem saying no. Hypothetical social committee member "Carl" is organizing the community's annual picnic. He is brainstorming for volunteers to help and thinks of Jennie. After all, she is very involved with many causes. Smartly, Carl asks Jennie if she would be able to purchase the paper goods for the event. He knows she won't say no, and this is a task that will not take a lot of time. If she fails, it is certainly easy enough to run out and buy paper goods at the last minute. Jennie is happy to be asked to do this manageable task and say her favorite word, "yes," and Carl has this task taken care of by someone who would be too busy to do another task. This is another win/win in the usage of volunteers.

The Burned-Out Board

Many associations have volunteers or board members who serve because they believe that they're the only ones that will do a job or can do it. In most cases, this is not true. See number 2 in the list at the beginning of the chapter. If the volunteers on your board and/or committees are doing their jobs for the sole reason that they don't think anyone else will be willing or able to do it, your association is most-likely not functioning to its highest potential. If that truly is the reason for these individuals' service, it is likely they are burned out and should face the fact that it's time to pass the baton. Each board should have a person or committee to actively nominate new members on a regular basis. It is refreshing for a board to have turnover on a regular basis, with staggered terms, so that new and seasoned members will be working together. The new members will bring energy to the group, and the experienced veterans will maintain the steady path while grooming the leadership for the future. It will also be a less daunting proposition to join the board or a committee if potential members are presented with a specified amount of time in which they'll serve, at the end of which they'll be given the option to rerun or step aside. No one wants to join anything that will basically be a life sentence.

16

Disaster Preparation

While every homeowner association hopes for a community that runs smoothly and safely, HOAs must remain aware of the possibility of disasters and dangerous situations in order to provide their residents with the greatest amount of safety and security. Thomas Engblom, CMCA, AMS, PCAM, VP/Regional Account Executive at Mutual of Omaha Bank outlined a plan of action for homeowner associations, detailing what to do prior to a disaster, and how to manage if disaster does indeed strike. Disasters can include anything from weather-related incidents, including hurricanes and tornadoes, to man-made disasters and emergencies, including bomb threats. While each scenario differs in how an HOA must react, there is a certain amount of preparation that an HOA may do to help ensure the well-being of its residents, first and foremost, and to help reduce damage to property.

Before enacting disaster preparation within an association, what exactly qualifies as a disaster? "A disaster is anything that would be unplanned," Engblom said. Some common disasters include fire, flood, tornado, electrical malfunction, etc., which of course vary in scale. "You should always plan for something that would be abnormal to your area as well. Planning for a disaster, geographically you may have fire, flood, or tornado, but you should prepare for the unknown." Consider any weather events that typically occur in your area, but also consider aspects of your surrounding area, including, for example, train tracks or chemical plants. Simply because a certain disaster or event has not occurred near an association or is quite rare, the association should still consider it a possibility and plan for it. Being over-prepared for a variety of disasters is a better plan of action than being completely unprepared. Bigger properties, with more units and residents, will need to prepare differently than smaller properties.

The Responsibility of the Association

Placing the burden of preparation entirely on the residents themselves is not an option. The association has a responsibility to its residents in the event of a disaster. The responsibility of the board is covered in the association's governing documents. "This goes back to the board, and the board is the governing agency. The board has a fiduciary responsibility to maintain the common elements. How do you maintain those common elements? They essentially need to restore the common elements to the condition that they were in before [the disaster]," Engblom said. "You want to protect the association, and the bigger concern is that you don't want any loss of life." To illustrate this, Engblom gave the example of an association where the power went out. The association did not want residents to walk up to their units in the dark through the stairwells because residents could injure themselves. In addition to jeopardizing the safety of residents, such a hazard could become a liability to the association.

Forming a Disaster Preparedness Plan

When actually planning for hypothetical disasters, Engblom suggested that associations prepare for different components of any problems that may arise. Additionally, disaster plans should be updated on a regular basis by trained professionals. Parties involved in the review process of a disaster plan include maintenance, management, the board of directors, or residents with a relevant skill set (fire personnel, tradespeople, medical personnel, etc.) to provide input. "You as a board member might not have the expertise, but if you call the fire department or the police department, they can give you insight to some of the basic information that would be a part of this." Engblom further noted that, if you have people involved in any of these fields within your own association, you can tap into their knowledge.

Insurance companies should be involved in the process as well. "You want to know how much they will cover and what authority you will have," Engblom said. The insurance company can provide the funds necessary, depending on the situation, to prevent any additional damage after the disaster. He advised that the association should first call 911 in the event of an emergency before contacting any other involved parties (including restoration or insurance companies).

Engblom also noted that FEMA (Federal Emergency Management Agency) provides information regarding disaster plans, including how to make a disaster preparedness kit and how to act both before and after a disaster occurs. They also provide booklets that can be kept by associations and their residents. The booklets cover a range of topics related to disaster preparedness, including what should be kept in preparedness kits — including water, flashlights, rope, plywood for boarding up windows, etc. Detailed information can be found on FEMA's website at www.fema.gov.

Associations should establish command centers to prepare prior to, and to coordinate following, the disaster. "A command center can be in the office or it can be in a different location so that everyone who is filtering through — such as contractors and emergency response personnel — can be briefed," Engblom said. In the emergency disaster plan you should also have a meeting place. "It can be down the street. Maybe it's at a church, maybe it's at a school. You want it conducive to your situation. You want people to go there and meet so that you can have a head count," Engblom said. Meeting locations may change depending on the season or the type of disaster. The main component is that the meeting place will serve as an information and treatment point as well as a refuge for residents.

Engblom noted the importance of establishing if any residents have special needs or circumstances that would be affected by certain situations. For example, if the power goes out and a resident needs an oxygen tank, having that knowledge on file allows the association to better

> **Preliminary Community Supply Checklist:**
>
> - First aid supplies
> - Emergency cordoning tape
> - Rope
> - Sheets and blankets
> - Battery-operated megaphone and whistles
> - Flashlights
> - Portable AM/FM radios
> - Walkie-talkies
> - Spare batteries and manual battery
> - Chargers
> - Flares
> - Poster board and markers
> - Blockades and flashing lights
> - Bottled drinking water
> - Water purification tablets
> - Non-perishable food
> - Camera
> - Plywood Sheets
> - Portable generators
> - Hygiene products
> - Filtering face masks
> - Tool kit
> - Plastic sheeting and duct tape

ensure that resident's safety. Associations should provide evacuation plans for residents and stipulate specific plans for non-ambulatory residents. If your association allows pets, provide a plan for them. Local pet hotels serve as a good option for boarding. Planning for every type of disaster requires that the association plan for the aftermath of every scenario as well.

Communication

Associations must also consider how to communicate information and updates to residents in the event of a disaster. Engblom said, "You may have a dedicated cable channel that you can utilize. You can call people at home, by cell phone, or email them." Automated technology that utilizes email or phone to send out blasts of information to certain groups of people is a good choice. This can be customized to fit the needs of your association as well. If a task force exists, they can be sent information specific to them while residents can be sent their own relevant information. Note that some lines of communication will cease functioning during certain scenarios (i.e. if there is a fire, updates by home phone is not the most efficient choice).

In order to best prepare residents, the association should have meetings to go over the disaster preparedness plan. They may also want to hold a mock-drill. Inform residents of the potential of upcoming events, such as fire drills and town hall meetings. Forms can be provided for residents to complete. "Consider having owners acknowledge receipt of the plan with a signature page," Engblom said. The plan can be included in association documents, such as the rules and regulations, and can be mailed out on an annual basis with a summer communications or annual meeting packet. Ensure that the plan is included in your resale disclosures.

In the event of a disaster, an association should hold meetings on a regular basis to keep residents informed and to discuss what damage has been addressed and how the situation should be dealt with. This harkens back to maintaining open lines of communication. "If you're with a management company, they will be the conduit for the communication that you have."

The Aftermath of the Disaster

Following a disaster, the association demonstrates their responsibility by liaising with a restoration company to repair any damage that occurred. The restoration process is discussed in detail in the next chapter, but here is a briefing of what typically should occur. If the disaster covered a wide area, a restoration company will need to prioritize a list of their own, which may delay repairs within your association. "The question becomes, do you have multiple restoration companies as a backup?" Engblom said. As will be detailed in the next chapter, associations should be prepared with information about restoration company contacts to help speed up the process of fixing any damaged common elements and returning the community to a place of normalcy.

Associations also should be aware of security issues and put measures in place to prevent burglaries if units will be unoccupied. "Call your vendors to make sure they are ready, willing, and able to perform board-up services and begin interior dry out," Engblom said. While security of your residents remains the priority, securing a building against theft helps to mitigate the stress following a disaster. Associations should further secure their important documents, including insurance policy documents, checks, owner lists, banking information, and a complete set of the governing documents.

As far as documentation of the disaster itself, associations need to report any damage to their insurance company. This process is detailed in Chapter 10 — Insurance. Briefly, the extent of documentation is done on a case by case basis and depends on the type of disaster, Engblom said. Insurance companies typically ask the date and time that the event occurred and what steps you are taking. Engblom recommended that you schedule an adjuster to call as soon as possible. If possible, require your restoration contractor or other vendor to meet with the adjuster on site to verify damage; try not to allow the adjuster to visit the site unaccompanied. Get the claim number as well as your insurance company contact's email address so that you can immediately follow-up with them, noting all of the information previously exchanged over the phone.

As part of preparing in advance, associations should catalog specific building information. Keep a file of the brand, model, and serial numbers of pumps, motors, appliances, swimming pools, and any other major equipment. Conduct a physical inventory of items such as furniture and equipment. Engblom added, "Videos of these items [before a disaster] will be invaluable."

The media may show up at an association in the event of a disaster. Engblom suggested letting a representative from the management company deal with the media, as they are more likely to have the expertise and the knowledge necessary to adequately address any questions. Engblom also suggested keeping the media off of the property, as they may only exacerbate ongoing problems.

While disasters can occur on a vast scale and vary greatly in type, associations do have the power to mitigate damage and panic to a certain extent. Preparing for a wide range of scenarios can help provide residents with a greater sense of security and can help the association fulfill its responsibility to the residents.

17

After the Disaster — Restoration of the Association

What happens when a property damage disaster occurs in an association? What steps need to be taken at the time of the disaster and afterwards in order to restore the property to its pre-disaster condition? Who is responsible for taking the necessary actions, the residents or the association? We spoke with Joshua Miller, CR, WLS, CMP of Concraft Restoration in Auburn Hills, Michigan to answer these questions.

Property damage events result in the destruction, ruin, and loss of possessions and property. However, the effects on a Property Manager, Association Board Members and the affected Co-Owners can reach much further than just the property involved. Due to this, individuals involved in such situations need to remember two common themes: the necessity to keep a level head under intense emotional stress and perceived chaos and they need to remember the difference that an experienced, qualified, certified restoration contractor can make.

Restoration companies handle clean-ups and repairs for a wide variety of disaster situations. These can include many different situations.

Anything from storm damage, such as shingles missing from a roof, siding that gets blown off the exterior, fires, floods and sump pump backup, to a car driving through a building or biohazard cleanup (such as situations where people pass away). Restoration companies have specialized training in a variety of restoration situations, such as smoke removal or determining when structural items should be replaced depending on how much char they have on them after a fire. They also have a unique knowledge and experience on how to properly clean and restore building materials and personal belongings that have been impacted by fire, smoke, soot, water, microbial growth, etc. A reconstruction or remodeling company, on the other hand, makes repairs, additions, and modifications to buildings without the added challenge of dealing with soot, char, microbial growth, etc. "A restoration company may appear to be the same as an everyday reconstruction company, however, the unique talents and abilities they bring to the table are invaluable in putting the structure back to its pre-loss condition," said Miller.

Emergency Response

If an association is experiencing any type of water damage, such as a broken water supply line in a common element, water damage from a fire suppression system, or if there is a hole in the roof due to storm damage, they should call a restoration company for emergency help. "We want to mitigate or prevent any secondary damage from the initial catastrophe," said Miller. He said that for an emergency, the company should be on-site within one hour from receiving that phone call. Arrival on site within one hour is a good guideline with regards to the Industry. He explained that in an emergency response, a company should get to the catastrophe as quickly as they can, do an assessment of the damage, and stabilize the site so that there's no more damage occurring. "You take into account the safety of any of the tenants, co-owners or building owners that might be there," he said. The company will also stabilize things to the point where an estimator can come in and prepare the repair estimate for the reconstruction company.

Who should the association call first, the restoration company, or their insurance company? Miller recommended calling the restoration company first to stabilize the damage and provide an assessment for repairs. "Many associations today have larger deductibles, $5,000 or $10,000, so before they submit an insurance claim, they should probably call the restoration company, allow the restoration company on-site to do their initial evaluation, perform any emergency services that need to be done, and then the restoration company can follow up with the association, either directly or through a property manager, to tell them what's going to be involved and give a rough estimate of the cost associated with what the repairs and mitigation would be," he said.

What's Next?

Once the site has been stabilized and evaluated by the restoration company the association can make the decision as to whether or not they want to file an insurance claim. Miller noted that the restoration company should be involved in every step of the process on behalf of the association. The association should give the insurance claim information to the restoration company, including the name of the insurance company, the claim number and the adjuster's contact information so the company can meet the adjuster on-site. The restoration company will then do a walk through with the adjuster and agree to the scope of work. The restoration company should also ensure the association's coverage is being maintained properly for the necessary repairs due to the damage.

Once the evaluation of the work is done, the restoration company will prepare an estimate for its work. Miller said this can take anywhere from a few hours to a couple weeks depending on the damage. Once prepared this is submitted to the insurance adjuster. The adjuster will review the estimate and call the restoration company with any observations, concerns or requests to the restoration company. "There is a negotiation process here to make sure everyone is on the same page," said Miller. Once the estimate is approved there is a dollar amount the restoration company can send on a contract to the association and have them sign for the exact dollar amount and scope of work that will be done.

The association needs to understand that the restoration company works directly for them and therefore the contract for work should be signed by the property manager and members of the association's board. "The restoration company is working for them, whereby the insurance company provides the insurance for the risk that they insure the association for," he said. The restoration company should meet with the insurance company so that an agreed upon scope of work can be created. Based upon that you will get an agreed upon amount of what the claim will cost. "The insurance company's legal or fiduciary responsibility is to the association. So once the insurance company has an agreed scope of work that they will pay off of, payment for the agreed dollar amount will be paid to the association," he said.

The association should check the dollar amount of the contract along with the payment terms for when the monies are due. Associations should also look at the terms for change orders. "Anything that's outside the scope of work that is listed in the initial agreement would require another written agreement for change orders or supplements along with signatures from all the necessary people so there are no surprises at the end," he said.

The Clean-up and Repairs

Once the contract is signed and returned, the restoration company will commence work. "Initially this will involve a pre-construction meeting with the Contractor's Project manager, the Association's Property Manager and any other necessary parties. At this meeting a review of the job scope should be discussed, selections made (such as paint color, carpet, cabinets, and countertops— anything cosmetically that needs to be selected) and any special circumstances discussed. After this meeting, all materials can be ordered, tradesmen scheduled, and an accurate job schedule can be created. With regard to material selections, many of these selections are dictated by the association's bylaws, but sometimes the co-owners are allowed to make these selections.

The work starts with any necessary demolition, deodorization or restoration, then after that any repair work would be done. "On a larger job that would be framing, the mechanicals, heating plumbing, electrical, then insulation, drywall and paint, cabinets, trim, carpet, right through the end," he said.

What the association should expect up front is a start to finish schedule from the restoration contractor, and then throughout the process there should be open, transparent communication between the contractor, the property manager and the association. This way the project should go smoothly, and any issues that are brought up by the co-owners, condo association and property manager can be dealt with promptly by the restoration company.

What is the role of the restoration company in regard to dealing directly with residents? The restoration company can communicate directly with anyone who has concerns. One caution is to make it clear to the co-owner that the restoration company is working for the association, many times through the property manager. "All final decisions regarding the scope of our work are developed from what the property manager or condo association tell us to do," said Miller. He said that many times co-owners are unclear about what they own or what the process is. So there needs to be open communication between the association, the property manager, the restoration company and the co-owners. One area this becomes apparent is with regard to damage in a co-owners unit that is their responsibility based on the association's bylaws. If the materials inside are a 'betterment or improvement,' the co-owner's HO-6 Insurance Policy would cover the cleaning, repair, and/or replacement of these materials.

Selecting a Restoration Company

The association doesn't need to wait for a disaster to happen to put the pieces in place in case one does. Restoration companies can be part of the disaster planning process for associations. The company can come in and instruct the association on who they should call if they have a water or fire event. They can also point out where all the water shut-offs and electric shut-offs are in the building. "So when something does happen, the on-site manager, property manager and condo board can all know what to do and who to call. Because once something does happen, there will be a lot of emotions involved," said Miller.

He pointed out that, depending on the severity of the loss, there could be a lot of chaos involving multiple co-owners. "That's not the time to be making a decision as to what contractor you want to do the work. It's better to do that upfront, when you can think things through, interview multiple contractors if necessary, and then set things up to get all emergency contact numbers and the names of people you should talk to," he said. A restoration company can take the lead in working all these things out for an association.

The choice of what restoration company to use is up to the owner of the property, not the insurance company. "The association has the right to choose whomever they want to do the work," said Miller. The insurance company can make recommendations, but outside of providing referrals, they have no role in selecting what company will perform the work. Miller highly recommended that the association make sure that the company they do select is an active member with the Restoration Industry Association (RIA). "The company performing the work would ideally have a Certified Restorer (CR) on staff, as this designation is the 'gold standard' of certification for restoration personnel. Other advanced designations are Water Loss Specialist (WLS) and Certified Mold Professional (CMP). Another organization that many respected restoration contractors belong to is the Institute of Inspection Cleaning and Restoration Certification (IICRC)," he said.

Common Misconceptions in Property Restoration

Miller said that the biggest misconceptions in disaster restoration stem from managing agent, board of directors, insurance adjusters, and co-owners not understanding the association's bylaws. Oftentimes, the parties involved in the repair process do not realize that the association is only responsible for the common elements. This can cause friction if Co-Owners do not understand where the association's insurance ends and their personal homeowner's policy begins.

He explained that many associations have a builder's standard-grade insurance policy. However, there are three known association policies that deal with Condo Associations that all parties should be aware of. ('Bare Walls' policy, Single Entity Policy, 'All In' Policy) Responsibilities and how they relate to different parties involved will depend to a large degree on the Insurance Policy that was purchased. The co-owners could have done a lot of upgrades to their unit after they purchased it, and if the Association has a 'single entity policy', when a catastrophe occurs the condo association only owes the co-owner for how their unit was the day it was purchased from the original builder. "That causes a lot of stress if the co-owners don't have proper insurance," he said. Those co-owners would need to pay out of pocket to restore their unit to include all of the upgrades, and this, according to Miller, causes them to be upset with the association, property manager or restoration company. So co-owners need to make sure their individual homeowner policies will adequately pick up where the association's insurance responsibility ends.

Another misconception is that the restoration work will start in just a few days following the damage causing incident. If it's a substantial loss, there are a lot of things that need to happen. In the case of a fire, for example, there needs to be an origin inspection for the cause of the fire and allowing the adjusters for all materially-interested parties to walk through the entire job site. This would include adjusters from not only the association's insurance company, but those from the co-owner's individual insurance policy's companies. "The process takes a little bit longer on the front end than a lot of people think it will," said Miller. Good communication, letting people know what to expect, is key to a successful restoration job.

How well the repairs to the damaged structure(s) within the Association proceed is largely up to the property manager and association board. Of course, the Contractor who performs the work must be qualified, skilled, and certified at the work they perform, but it is the job of the property manager to communicate exactly what they expect during the job. If you are not sure, make sure to ask plenty of questions and do not move on until you understand the information given as an answer. Through good communication, patience, transparency, and trust, an emotionally stressful and overwhelming situation can be handled promptly and professionally with great results for all parties involved.

18

The Association's Roofs

It's not something one thinks about on a daily basis — in fact, if functioning properly, most people take their home's roof for granted. That being said, when you do think about it, a well-performing roof is a highly important component of an association — and many times roofs are one of the community's common elements. We spoke with Steve McCusker from Roof One in Pontiac Michigan about how to maximize the life of your association's roof and ensure it's doing its job. While roof replacement is a major capital project for the association, when you think about what the roof does, you get tremendous value from properly installing and maintaining the roofs, rather than taking the bottom-line cheapest route on maintenance, repairs and replacements. "Per square foot, roofing is typically the least expensive thing that is done to the home," said McCusker. He noted it costs more per square foot to install hardwood flooring, a bathroom or a kitchen than it does to install a roof that protects everything in your house.

He made the point that associations can lessen the possibility of roof problems by doing their due diligence, having professionals do the proper and necessary inspections and maintenance, and not making choices based on the lowest initial cost.

Protecting and Maintaining the Roof

How can HOAs assure their roofs are prepared for bad weather? "Annual inspections should be done on the roofs," said McCusker, "checking for loose gutters and downspouts, making sure the gutters are cleaned, that there are no loose shingles or flashings and making sure flashings are proper."

What should an association expect to happen during a typical inspection? An association should receive a complete detail analysis for the life expectancy of a shingle — what is left in it. The inspection should also detail what is left in the roof flashings and gutters. Also the attic inspection should be part of this process, making sure the soffits are open and the vents are vented to the outside and not back into the attics. Possible siding issues should also be looked at.

McCusker recommended that HOAs develop a relationship with a roofing company that does annual or biannual inspections of the roof. They should also have a company that runs a repair department that is on call 24-hours a day for emergencies. This company should be able to send someone out within two hours of receiving an emergency call regarding the roof.

One major seasonal issue that affects roofs, gutters and siding are winter ice dams. How do these occur? Some of the reasons for ice dam formation are improper ventilation, inadequate insulation, builder's design and, of course, mother nature. "The sun just doesn't pop up over houses and melt roof snow evenly," said McCusker. Shaded areas, due to the way a home is constructed, trees, etc., are going to melt off last, and whatever is above it is going to come down and create the ice dam. Also, if there is inadequate insulation in the attic, it can cause the attic space and the roof

> **During heavy snowfall or an ice storm, should snow be removed from roofs?**
>
> In winters with several snowstorms and lots of accumulations, snow should be removed from eave edges, which is typically done by a snow rake. Make sure that whoever is doing it is a roofing professional. Otherwise they could end up damaging the roof.

above it to become too warm from the heat in the house, causing melting which can pool on the roof. Ultimately, ice dams will cause leaks due to the water pooling or backing up.

We typically think of roof problems occurring in winter, however summer has its issues as well. McCusker cautioned against walking on the roof during very hot weather, as it can ruin the roof shingles. "If the roof is too hot and you're walking on it, you're pressing down on the granules in the asphalt into the matting. When asphalt gets extremely hot it's pliable," he said. So having maintenance done to the roof or gutter cleaning where workers need to walk on the roof in extreme heat is not a good idea.

Not every roof issue involves a major repair. Some minor repairs that come up are repairs to flashings, chimney flashings that have come loose, or wind damage. Additionally, sometimes flashings around plumbing stacks on the roof create leaks in the neoprene or where the rubber is cracked. McCusker said that digital photos can be taken to find where the water is coming in and also show that the repair has been made properly.

Again, the best way for associations to protect their property is to have annual inspections done on the roofs in spring, after the winter, or in autumn right after the leaves have dropped. Also very important — in the fall associations should make sure the gutters have been cleaned and the building is all set for winter.

If an association notices a leak or damage on their own, McCusker doesn't recommend unqualified people going onto the roof to try to

Watch the Water Run

You should make sure that water doesn't run from a gutter onto another roof. This is something that would reduce the life expectancy of the shingles below. Improper gutter downspouts could even affect a building's foundation if the downspout is not draining properly.

It is important to make sure gutters are cleaned out, typically in spring and fall, and they should not be loose. Anything from the gutters up are part of a maintenance program for the roofing. This includes any siding that is built up to a second level from one roof up.

cover the area. He advises associations to wait for a professional to come out. He said that if the association does have a knowledgeable individual on staff, that person can go up and tarp the damaged area, but otherwise, he said not to do anything until the roofer arrives. Improper tarping can cause issues in another area, or the individual could end up injuring himself.

Planning for Roof Replacements

Planning for how long a roof will last, and how much it will cost to replace depends on what the association has on their roofs to begin with. "They should have money set aside for roof replacements depending on what shingles they have on the roof," said McCusker. He noted that basically insurance companies say that a roof should last 18 years. However, McCusker said that the new roof systems, with proper installation and ventilation, should last longer than that — possibly 20-25 years.

So what is the process for replacing the roofs? McCusker explained that you need to have a professional do an assessment of the roof, the ventilation and the attic space — that's all done first so that you can establish the specifications. Also, associations should plan to have the work done on a time line so that the roofs will be installed during the proper weather. "The temperature needs to be above 45 degrees with sunlight for the proper sealing," he said. Typically, the time between spring and fall is optimal.

The association can then send those specifications out to companies as a request for proposals (RFP). McCusker said that RFPs should specify the scope of work, job completion dates, cancellation clauses, workmanship warranties, materials to be used, proper insurance — both workers' compensation and general liability — cleanup expectancies, ventilation plans and more. "If they want the roof to last it's not just the person who can get up there the fastest with the cheapest materials, with the cheapest labor," he said. They need to replace all of the flashings, make sure it's vented properly, make sure baffles are in place in the attic so that air passes through, and make sure that it's a bound system from eave to ridge.

So in reviewing the various RFPs from different companies, can associations be sure they're comparing apples to apples, so to speak? You really can't, said McCusker. "Unless it's a speced job, where all materials are listed, all workmanship areas are listed, that's really the only way you can compare apples to apples. And then you're relying on the labor, whether it's the same qualified labor or not," he said.

Once the work begins, the association doesn't need to be involved in the process, but McCusker noted that they should make a work order if they notice any damage and follow through to make sure the repair is addressed, making sure to obtain proper paperwork all the way through.

And what about those roof warranties? According to McCusker, the best warranties are those backed by a manufacturer. These warranties would cover workmanship, materials, labor and total roof replacement. As far as the materials themselves, fiberglass asphalt shingles are the most popular materials being used. There are different grades and it is important to choose the correct one for the needs of a particular building.

In a nutshell, McCusker said the most important things to pay attention to are the materials being used, warranties on those materials and the professionalism of the company installing roof. If associations do this, they will be far better off than just looking for a cheap bid. "It all costs money to do a job right," he said.

Glossary

Accounts Payable - the debts of the association to be paid

Accounts Receivable - monies due to the association, including assessments

Accrual Basis Accounting - accounting method that records income when it is earned (or assessed to owners in the case of condo or homeowners associations) and expenses when they are incurred or acquired, such as when an invoice is issued to the association.

Arbitration - when a third party is entrusted to make a ruling in a dispute based on the information provided

Assessment - proportionate share of what a co-owner pays for maintenance fees, expenses or reserves on an annual basis

Audit - the highest review of accounting procedures and practices; an accountant must issue a management opinion, representation, and engagement before proceeding; follows the GAAP rule (Generally Accepted Accounting Procedures)

Betterments and Improvements - upgrades to a condominium unit as it was originally sold by the developer. These include bathroom fixtures, cabinets, built-ins, upgraded carpet, and any other items that would remain with the unit if sold

Budget - a projection of the association's income and expenses for a fiscal year

Business Judgement Rule - a rule specifying that courts should defer to the decisions of the board of an association, when the board has upheld, fulfilled and acted within its fiduciary duties

Bylaws - the administrative functionality of the association in written format

Capital Project - a construction project intended for the improvement or maintenance of large items (i.e. roofing, paving, siding)

Cash Basis Accounting - accounting method that records income when it is collected and expenses when they are paid.

Cash Value - referring to an insurance loss, the replacement cost of an item, minus depreciation

Chart of Accounts - a listing or description of all the line items within the budget (i.e. assessments, water, electric, etc.)

Civil Rights - the protection of a citizen's political and social freedoms

Common Elements (Common Areas) - areas in a community that are owned by everyone, based on percentage of ownership (i.e. lawn, hallway, pool, etc.)

Condominium Association - an entity consisting of percentage of ownership and the legal rights that occur when a person purchases within that entity; typically lien-based, have mandatory membership, and have binding documents

Co-owner - each resident who has a percentage of ownership within a particular property so that total ownership equals 100%

Construction Defect- a detrimental condition existing due to an error made during construction

Developer - an individual who buys land and then comes up with a plan for a property, subdivision, or communal environment; puts the property together based on the architectural design and sells the units as they are built

Fiduciary Duty - an obligation for board members of the association to act in the best interest of the association and not place personal goals ahead of those of the association

Financial Statement - a formal report of the financial activities of the association over a specified period of time

Foreclosure - the judicial and physical remedy for the bank or association to take back a property where the owner has a mortgage on which they have stopped making payments

Garnishment - a court order for collecting on a monetary judgement that enables the association to take a percentage of a delinquent resident's earned wages to satisfy their debt

Homeowner Association - a master association for the exterior of the property with subdivisions that divide it; it takes care of anything that pertains to the exterior of the property (i.e. pool, clubhouse, landscaping, facilities)

Judgment - a court order issued by a judge on the possession or monetary amount based on a ruling

Major Improvement - a construction project intended for the addition of an item to an association (i.e. pool, tennis court)

Master Deed - a document that gives control over all of the sub-phases of a property that has multiple phases; the starting point of the homeowners association

Modified Cash Basis Accounting - accounting method that records income and expenses on a cash basis with selected items recorded on an accrual basis

Operating Account (Operating Fund) - daily checking account to be used for the functionality of the association's accounts receivable and accounts payable

Proxy - the authority to cast another resident's vote or to represent a resident in a meeting

Replacement Value - in reference to an insurance loss, the amount to replace an item to its present-day, pre-loss condition

Reserve Study - the physical and financial review of all the components of the property in an association, performed to determine a plan for reserve funding

Restoration - after a disaster or emergency, bringing a damaged property back to a condition similar to its original one, whether by repairing or replacing

Self Insure - in instances where it is possible to purchase insurance for a particular purpose, and the association decides not to purchase that insurance, they therefore are self insuring for that purpose.

Special Assessment - a levy placed upon your account, additional income, or services/fees required by the association not within the budget

Statute (statutory) - a law (according to law)

Subdivision Plan - goes back to the master deed, where smaller properties can be established within the master division of the property

The Sources

Following is some brief information about the individuals we interviewed in writing this book. These people were an invaluable resource of information on the many important topics that fill these pages. The names are sorted alphabetically by last name.

Scott Breslin

Scott Breslin graduated from Albion College in Michigan with a degree in Economics and Management. He joined the McCredie Agency, Inc., located in Flint, MI, in 1996. Since then, he has worked in the field of commercial and professional risk management, and his speciality is in condominium and apartment insurance. An avid golfer, Breslin understands the benefit of helping young people develop the skills necessary to succeed in the business world. Many of those skills can be learned on the golf course. The Trusted Choice® Big "I" National Championship is the nation's largest junior stroke-play golf tournament and also one of the premier junior golf events. The event, organized by the Independent Insurance Agents & Brokers of America (The Big "I"), attracts elite junior golfers from forty-three states. As a supporter of this event, Breslin has served on the planning committee for the Michigan chapter since 2003. He was State Chair from 2005-2008. Currently, he serves on the board of the Flint Junior Golf Association (FJGA). The FJGA is one of the oldest junior golf programs in the country. In 2000, Breslin was recognized as the Young Agent of the Year by the Young Agents Council, a division of the Michigan Association of Insurance Agents (MAIA), which is the largest Association in Michigan for the Independent Insurance Agents, representing independent agencies and industry employees. An active member of the United Condominium Owners of Michigan (UCOM) and Community Associations Institute (CAI) Michigan Chapter, Breslin has been a frequent lecturer at conferences on the importance of liability coverage for homeowners associations for the last seven years. Breslin currently resides in Grand Blanc, MI, and he is currently pursuing his Certified Insurance Counselor designation.

Thomas C. Engblom, CMCA, ARM, AMS, CPM, PCAM

Thomas C. Engblom, CMCA, ARM, AMS, CPM, PCAM entered the field of real estate in 1984 as a licensed real estate broker/instructor in Illinois and taught as a university professor at numerous colleges and universities during the same period. Since 2004, Engblom has taught as a National Instructor for Community Associations Institute (CAI), including assisting in rewriting several of their Professional Management Development Program (PMDP) course materials. Furthermore, Engblom served on the National Business Council for CAI. Engblom has formerly supervised 3,500 condominium units within Chicago, IL and its suburbs for twenty years with two management firms. Engblom began working as an Association Banker for Mutual of Omaha Bank in 2004. He is a regional account executive for Mutual of Omaha Bank's Community Association Banking group. He serves seven states in the northern Midwest region, consisting of Minnesota, Wisconsin, Illinois, Indiana, Michigan, Kentucky and Ohio. Within those territories, he serves on the CAI Board of Directors in Minnesota, Illinois and Michigan.

Engblom has consistently placed among the top performers in five categories throughout the entire bank organization. He was also one of ten individuals honored out of nearly 1,000 bank employees nationwide. Mutual of Omaha awarded Engblom with the company's Pillar Award, which is an honor given annually to the bank's top 10 performers nationwide. Additionally, Engblom has earned the Certified Property Manager (CPM) designation from the Institute of Real Estate Management (IREM) and the Professional Community Association Manager (PCAM) designation from CAI. Engblom is currently completing his Doctorate in Business Administration with his Dissertation dedicated to Association Management.

Mark F. Makower, Esq.

Mark F. Makower, Esq., is a founding partner at Makower Abbate and Associates, PLLC, located in Farmington Hills, MI, which focuses on real estate development and construction law. In this capacity, Makower handles all aspects of community association/development law from feasibility and financing through project documentation, construction and sales, and representation of community associations. He has been involved in the creation of more than 100 condominiums statewide and participated in the revision and correction of documentation, including litigation, for several hundred other developments. He now represents several dozen developers, numerous trades, and over 1,000 community associations statewide, handling resolution of construction defects/disputes, operational responsibilities and issues, document enforcement and amendment, collections, policy formulation and practical advice. He also counsels self-managed and professionally managed complexes, working with more than 65 different management companies. Makower has had numerous speaking and teaching engagements throughout the state of Michigan and has written for legal journals and publications nationwide. Makower is the only community association lawyer in Michigan to be accepted as a fellow in the American College of Real Estate Lawyers (ACREL) and is only one of 2 Michigan attorneys accepted into the College of Community Association Lawyers (CCAL). In his time as an attorney, he received the Excellence in Public Policy and Governmental Affairs Award from CAI National and CAI-Michigan's President Award. He was selected as a Michigan Super Lawyer, a *DBusiness* Top Lawyer and a Leading Lawyer. He has been awarded numerous other awards and recognition of merit from organizations and councils that include CAI National and the Michigan Chapter, Habitat for Humanity and others. Makower currently serves as a member of the CAI-Michigan Board of Directors and has served in the past both as the chapter's president and vice president and has served on the CAI National Amicus Curiae Brief writing team. He also serves as co-chair of the Legislative Action Committee (LAC) for CAI-Michigan. Makower has been a member of the chapter since its inception in 1998.

Steve McCusker

Steve McCusker is a roofing specialist at Roof One, located in Pontiac, MI. Roof One is a Platinum Preferred Contractor (one of 100 such qualified contractors across the country) with Owens Corning, a Presidential Master Elite Contractor with GAF, and a Select Shingle Master with Certainteed. Jim Nelle has been in the roofing business since 1984, and he began Roof One in 2001 with McCusker. As joint owners of Roof One, Jim Nelle and Steve McCusker provide quality workmanship, materials, and guarantees, along with a variety of siding types and installation, window replacement, gutter systems, and blown-in insulation. Roof One continually invests in training and certifying their employees. The company has now been in business for twenty-six years. During his time as a roofing specialist, McCusker has earned various certificates and distinctions, including the completion of the Owens Corning Total Protection Roofing System Contractor Education Module, the Vinyl Siding Institute Certified Installer Program, the Owens Corning Asphalt Shingles: Types, Testing and Compliance Program, and the Air Vent's Attic Ventilation: Ask the Expert Seminar. McCusker has also completed the 2009 TruSlate Pro Field Guide Test and the Rodney Webb Superstar Sales Force Recruiting and Training Session. In 2012, he completed the CARE - Most Common Mistakes course. Additionally, McCusker has earned the distinction of Certainteed Building Solutions Specialist.

Joshua Miller, CR, WLS, CMP

Joshua Miller, CR, WLS, CMP has been in the Restoration and Cleaning industry for the past 18 years. During that time he has held numerous positions that have dealt with all phases of the restoration process. He holds numerous advanced technical designations within in the industry. These include such designations as the Institute of Inspection Cleaning and Restoration (IICRC) Master Textile Cleaner, IICRC Master Water Restorer, and IICRC Master Fire and Smoke Restorer. Additionally, Miller has attained all three of the Restoration Industry Associations' (RIA) highest designations, including Certified Restorer (CR), Water Loss Specialist (WLS), and Certified Mold Professional (CMP). After working with numerous companies across North America helping them to refine their restoration systems to improve results and productivity, Miller currently serves as the General Manager of a dynamic restoration firm in Southeast Michigan that specializes in working to help multi-family communities recover and restore after property damage disasters.

John P. Poehlmann, RS

John P. Poehlmann, RS, Principal, is a co-founder of Reserve Advisors, Inc. Poehlmann received a Master of Science Management from the University of Wisconsin-Milwaukee and a Bachelor of Business Administration from the University of Wisconsin. He is responsible for the finance, accounting, marketing, and overall administration of Reserve Advisors, Inc. He also regularly participates in internal Quality Control Team Reviews of reserve study reports. Poehlmann directs corporate marketing, including business development, advertising, press releases, conference exhibiting, and direct mail promotions. He frequently speaks throughout the country at seminars and workshops on the benefits of future planning and budgeting for capital repairs and replacements of building components and other assets. Poehlmann served on the national Board of Trustees of Community Associations Institute (CAI) and is a member of multiple chapters. He is a founding member of CAI's Reserve Committee, which developed national standards and the Reserve Specialist (RS) Designation Program for Reserve Study providers. Poehlmann has authored numerous articles on the topic of Reserve Studies for a variety of publications, including the *Chicago Tribune, The Milwaukee Journal/Sentinel, Common Ground, Common Interest,* and *Condo Management.* He also coauthored "Reserves," an educational videotape produced by Reserve Advisors on the subject of Reserve Studies and the benefits of maintaining appropriate reserves. The videotape is available through Reserve Advisors or CAI's website, www.caionline.org and libraries in the State of Virginia. Poehlmann has received the CAI National Rising Star Award, the CAI Michigan Chapter Award, and 2014 Excellence Award from the CAI Wisconsin Chapter. Poehlmann is a member of the Association of Condominium, Townhouse & Homeowners Associations.

Linda R. Strussione, CPA

Linda Strussione, President of Owens & Strussione, P.C., located in Shelby Township, MI, is a member of the American Institute of Certified Public Accountants (AICPA), the Michigan Association of Certified Public Accountants (MACPA), The Michigan Chapter of Community Associations Institute (CAI) and United Condominium Owners of Michigan (UCOM). Since 2008, she has served as a volunteer committee member on the CAI-Michigan Legislative Action Committee. Owens & Strussione, P.C.'s professional client portfolio consists of approximately 180 condominium, cooperative housing, and homeowners associations that range in size up to 691 units, as well as many corporate clients in various industries. Strussione has been with the firm for thirty-one years, becoming the owner in 1992. In this capacity, she performs audits, reviews and tax related work. She also does corporate consulting, represents clients for IRS audits, litigation support, and developer conflict issues. Strussione has taught for UCOM and CAI seminars on subjects including reserve funding, budgets, audits, and accounting.

Robert A. Travis, CIRMS, CPIA

Robert A. Travis, CIRMS, CPIA, has been the Vice President/National Marketing Director/Regional Marketing Director for Community Association Underwriters (CAU) for more than 19 years, where he draws upon 36 years' experience in the commercial insurance industry. Travis has been the insurance agent for over 1,000 community associations since 1986 and is currently licensed to write insurance programs for community associations in thirty states. Travis has also done consulting and educational work for community associations, property managers and insurance agents in 10 additional states. For CAU, Travis currently oversees the company's entire direct sales, business development and customer service operations. Prior to joining CAU, Travis held various positions at Engle, Hambright & Davies (EH&D), C.M. Stauffer Insurance, Crum & Forster Insurance Companies, Continental Insurance Group, Rasmussen Administrators, and Western Employers. Travis is a former member of both Community Associations Institute's (CAI) National Board of Trustees and the Business Partners Council Board. Travis has served on the CAI Chapter Boards for the CAI Pocono Mountain/Northeast Pennsylvania Chapter and the CAI Pennsylvania and Delaware Valley Chapter. He served as President for the former from 1993-1994 and for the latter in 2013. Travis has earned several awards for his work with CAI, including the CAI Chapter Distinguished Service to Communities Award in 2003, CAI Chapter Volunteer of the Year in 2000, and CAI Council Business Partner of the Year in 2004. Travis was also the recipient of American Resort Development Association's (ARDA) Ace Innovator of the Year in 2001. He has been a member of CAI's national faculty for 16 years, teaching basic and advanced Risk Management and Insurance classes. He was named CAI's Educator of the Year in 2001 and 2009. As an educator, Travis also teaches classes that have been recognized by Departments of Insurance of the Commonwealth of Pennsylvania and the State of New Jersey for Continuing Education Credits for Insurance Agents. Travis holds a Bachelor of Science degree from Jacksonville University in Jacksonville, FL, and his post-graduate work in Public and Business Administration was done at Farleigh Dickinson University in Madison, NJ.